STOP TALKING AND
GIVE THE SCORE

MAX ROBERTSON

STOP TALKING AND GIVE THE SCORE

[*Spice of Life*

Mr. Max Robertson,
  Mr. Georgie Wood,   Sir Alan Herbert,   Mr. Jack Train

THE KINGSWOOD PRESS

The Kingswood Press
an imprint of William Heinemann Ltd
10 Upper Grosvenor Street, London WIX 9PA
LONDON   MELBOURNE
JOHANNESBURG   AUCKLAND

Copyright © 1987 by Max Robertson

First published 1987
0 434 98085 4

Photoset by Deltatype, Ellesmere Port
Printed and bound by in Great Britain by
Mackay's of Chatham

For Liza and Nancy and our children – with love

CONTENTS

	AUTHOR'S PREFACE	ix
1	WIMBLEDON FAREWELL	1
2	A POMMY IN PAPUA	19
3	I TAKE TO THE AIR	29
4	THE END OF AN ERA	38
5	'GOING BUSH'	47
6	DOWN THE CRESTA	57
7	NEW FRONTIERS	65
8	THESE I HAVE KNOWN	71
9	COMING 'HOME'	80
10	STATE OCCASIONS	86
11	FREELANCE AT A VENTURE	96
12	PANORAMA	102
13	SPORTING OCCASIONS	114
14	COMMONWEALTH VISION – A CHILDREN'S CRUSADE	128
15	GOING FOR A SONG	136
16	INSIDER OUTSIDE	146
	EPILOGUE	154
	INDEX	159

AUTHOR'S PREFACE

IN WRITING THIS MEMOIR I'VE BEEN PARTICULARLY INDEBTED TO THREE PEOPLE, MY SECRETARY, MY EDITOR AND MY INSPIRATION. The first, Liz Watts, has her own very busy life in Guernsey – as a wife and mother, as a school secretary in the morning, and in the summer running her own tea-garden in one of the Island's attractive bays. It was because she saw it as a challenge that she agreed to come for two hours a day from September to Christmas last year. Using a word processor we managed it, though sometimes the processor, particularly when my vacuum cleaner manipulated the software, drove us to despair. I shall be eternally grateful to Liz for her loyalty, hard work, punctuality, regularity, good humour, and ability with synonyms.

As to Derek Wyatt, any of his many other authors will recognise his editorial style – and feel for me – as I pay tribute to him. He it was who set the acute deadline for this donkey; who then, dissatisfied with what I had sent him as my opening chapters, suggested the book ought to start with my last day in the commentary box at Wimbledon (he was right, of course); who has alternately condemned and cajoled, provoked and soothed; criticized and faintly praised; and finally taken unto me his favourite stick, Mary Lou Grimberg. Between them I have been beaten into submission and am now completely docile, allowing them to have their ruthless way with my words, those drops of blood shed to the processor.

In all seriousness, between them they have done a superb job and, if in the end this book does find any favour, it will be entirely due to their professionalism for which I am truly grateful. If, on the other hand, it languishes unrequited, I shall know, too, where the responsibility lies, feeling completely absolved myself. It seems to me that's not a bad each-way bet.

I'm also grateful to Margot Richardson, Kingswood's house editor, for her charming but watchful eye over the production; to Sue Hadden for her expert and sympathetic work with the illustrations; to Claudia Zeff for producing such an eye-catching jacket; to Rachel Ward Lilley for her zestful and resourceful promotion of the book; and also to Louise Hidalgo, Derek's secretary, who did her best to soften the severity of his strictures.

My especial thanks go to my old friend and commentator colleague, Norris McWhirter, at whom I quick-fired various esoteric points that I needed to check. As I expected, he was able to supply many of the answers straight out of his head, or by reaching for one of the multifarious reference books I knew he would have to hand. For others he put his faithful bloodhound, Colin Smith, on to the track and my thanks go to him, too.

I must record my particular appreciation and thanks to John Gaisford, who laboured long and imaginatively, refusing reward for his good nature, to produce manifold negatives and prints from my scrap-books, so that they could be used for the jacket and in montage for the end papers. He also did a rush job of many of the prints, from which the final selection of illustrations was made.

Finally, my wholehearted gratitude goes to my 'inspiration', Pat Savill, who throughout the terrible gestation was my saviour, support and per se distraction. The challenge of Derek has been considerable but her's even more important. I felt it vital to get the job done – to prove myself to her.

ARMAINE, ST. PETER PORT C.I.

1ST JANUARY 1987

1

WIMBLEDON FAREWELL

IT IS SUNDAY 6 JULY 1986, THE DAY OF THE MEN'S FINAL AT
WIMBLEDON. IT IS ALSO MY LAST DAY OF SOME 500 IN THIS SEAT – ONE
of the best outside the royal box that you could find on the Centre
Court. And it is a very unreal feeling.

I have come in early to take my accustomed place at the righthand
end of the front row of the commentators' box. Three can sit in this
row; two more can sit on the bench behind, but having five people
in that small enclosed space is overwhelming, leading to lack of
oxygen in the brain when one is trying to concentrate on what is
perhaps one of the fastest radio commentaries performed anywhere. It's always on finals' days that there is most pressure on the
box. More of the team are needed than usual, so I hope that on this,
my last day, no 'friends' will drop in for the ride.

Thinking of this reminds me of an occasion, just after the war,
when I was sharing commentary with Rex Alston. He was talking
when there was rather a noisy entrance and a distinguished looking
man, with a familiar face, came in and sat down at the back. I gave
the visitor a reproving look, which he blandly ignored. In those
days we were always having it impressed on us that nobody
unconnected with a broadcast should ever be in the box. It was 'bad
form', which the secretary of the club, Colonel Macaulay, was
known to frown upon. After a while I looked round again. The
man was still there, so again I frowned. Not long after, it was my
turn to commentate and I was soon immersed in the match, though
I was aware when the intruder left us. At a pause in play, I raised my
eyes to the Royal Box to describe the occupants and found myself

1

looking straight at our recent visitor – Earl Mountbatten of Burma.

My colleagues have over the years kindly allowed me to sit here on the right of the line, even when producers' whims and quirks have swapped us around from court to court and I have come back for the second or third match. I suppose an old dog likes his corner by the fire. Actually, although slightly straighter on to the court than the lefthand seat which the alternate commentator uses, mine does not allow me to see the players' friends and coaches without deliberately leaning forward and getting 'off mike'.

I've come up much sooner than usual to savour and garner the atmosphere on my last day. My colleagues – broadcasters, engineers, and secretaries alike – today seem to show a silent sympathy during my 'last rites' and have been artificially normal. There have been the usual telephone calls as requests for specialised pieces for News or other programmes come in. The build-up introduction to the afternoon's programme, a montage of excerpts from past commentaries and interviews, was already being shaped by expert hands. Tony Adamson, normally a fine commentator on Wimbledon, has this year been the presenter of the programme with Peter Jones away on duty at the World Cup. Tony was busy writing cues in the little presentation cubicle, occasionally getting information or instruction from the director on his headphones. Various people closely connected – and some not so closely – with our broadcasting set-up, were drifting in and out of the control point bringing messages, seeking contacts or just rubbernecking. It was all part of the everyday Wimbledon scene except that, as there was only the Centre Court involved, there was less complication than normal.

I got away from this as soon as possible – to be alone with my thoughts and preparation. It's a short walk from the control point across the South West Hall to the wooden companionway that leads to our Centre Court platform. The original control point had been housed in a secondhand telephone box, which had been sold to the BBC for £5. It had stood near the foot of the wooden stairway. It was still in use just after the war – a considerable contrast to the present-day hub of our operation that I've just left. Now it's about ten steps up and then a left turn that brings me to the small aperture giving access to the box platform. This is one 'facility' that has not been improved since the position was first enlarged to accommodate foreign broadcasters in 1934.

Even a young person can find this a little difficult to negotiate until the technique is mastered. Mine, evolved over the years, is to put my right foot on the small stair, stretch my left out over the step of the concrete edge as if I were hurdling it, duck under and up in one swift movement and emerge like a submariner from the hatch of a conning-tower. It always worried me that one day I might not be able to do this with sufficient ease and that might be a sign that I was getting too old for the job. A year or two ago Ted Tinling, who is very tall, had to come up for an interview and found it very difficult. In the end he struggled through somehow, but it was not in his usual dignified manner. After this the BBC radio sports powers tried to get the hole enlarged but met with an adamant refusal, since it might have affected the vital integrity of the Centre Court structure. Fortunately my method works well on this my last time.

The Centre Court is still looking its brilliant self, though the first day's immaculate perfection of emerald green has long weathered and worn. One or two of the groundstaff are preparing the umpire's chair and an electrician is testing the microphones. Some more boxes of balls are being packed into the green refrigerated box; the drinks receptacle at the umpire's chair is being filled and so is the resin box. Jim Thorn, that magician of grass, is drifting around in his by now mandatory white cap and with familiar cigarette drooping from his lips. The referee, Alan Mills, comes onto the court to exchange a word with him and palm the grass for 'feel'. The duty policeman is having a little backchat with one or two early arrivals in the open courtside seats. There are still not many people in the covered stands, though even there some have preferred to bring in a picnic lunch, listen to the band and sniff the air as I am doing.

My mind wanders back over the years, trying to remember and evaluate the changes of scene. How many years now since the all-electric scoreboard came in? How long ago since the digital clock became a component of the scoreboard and remorselessly replaced the old familiar moon-faced one, diagonally opposite from my seat – my seat which I have always tried to share with you, the listeners, rejoicing with you that we have one of the best positions in the Centre Court, just to the left of the Royal Box and right in the thick of the atmosphere? I used to like to time the matches by that clock, now effaced by an All-England Club emblem. It was just to the side of where the groundsmen had by ancient right one or two bench seats in front of the old roller, whose shafts stuck up into the air like the pincers of a stag beetle. The roller itself had been a favourite vantage point for some of the groundsmen's friends. Last year it was relegated to behind the stop-netting, so that more proper rows

3

of seats could be built into the corner. Then its shafts had still been forlornly visible above the backcloth, but now even they had been lowered and the roller, so long a character of the court which had been built around it and forced it to remain there, is lost to sight. I have a distinct fellow-feeling for the roller today – especially as years ago, in order to distinguish someone playing from 'the end opposite the Royal Box' (rather a clumsy phrase for constant repetition) I christened it the 'Roller End'. I wonder if now that name will stick with a new generation of commentators?

As I am pondering these thoughts and doodling in my scorebook I look up to see that a couple of the groundsmen under Jim's command are rolling the umpire's chair out from the courtside to its officiating position on court. They stop and Jim queries me with a questioning thumbs-up to ask if my sight of the far lefthand tramline is affected at all. The chair needs to go back a foot or so and he gives his men the nod. This is a little arrangement I have had for many years with the head groundsman and one that makes such a difference to the commentator's judgment of a close call.

While that's happening another figure starts busying himself on court. I realise suddenly that this is the man in charge of Cyclops, the 'magic eye' which since 1980 has been the arbiter of service-line faults. I'm rather hazy as to exactly what it does and seize my chance to brush up. He tells me that the electronic beam runs from approximately one-eighth of an inch on the wrong side of the service-line to a depth of eighteen inches. Any ball touching the ground within the beam automatically sets up a bleep denoting a fault.

Now I am getting my scorebook ready for this final match, the names of Lendl, the world number one and Becker, the reigning champion as headings across the page; and underneath each name the relevant facts I need for my commentary. To the left are the columns in which I show the server and the game scores standing to each man. I enter the records of their previous meetings and achievements and there is no more I can do for the moment. Again my mind starts wandering back – this time over the forty-one years and finals I have seen and described – and the great players who have strutted (and some fretted on) this superb stage.

For example, the tall Frenchman, Yvon Petra, in 1946 the last 'white flannelled fool' to win the title in long trousers and who in victory – gained after a titanic fight – had comforted Geoff Brown with a marvellous bearhug; the great Jack Kramer, an outstanding

4

tennis machine; the artistic and elegant Budge Patty; twinkle-toed Frank Sedgman of the incisive volley; Jaroslav Drobny, 'Drob' the crowd's heart-throb of the wide grin and little adjustment to his spectacles, who beat Ken Rosewall in the first of the Aussie's four losing finals over twenty years; Kenny himself, the most perfectly poised player, with his immaculate backhand; Rosewall's 'twin' Lew Hoad, one of the most gifted, powerful and dramatic players ever; Neale Fraser, a strong if not so talented lefthanded champion, now the Harry Hopman of today's Australian Davis Cup squad; Rod Laver, the 'Rocket', one of the greatest champions of all and lefthanded also; and yet more Australians, Roy Emerson and John Newcombe, the last in their long line of dominance.

The seventies had seen Americans and one Swede in command. Of the first the most formidable had undoubtedly been Pancho Gonzales, who had only played once at Wimbledon in his hey-day – in 1949. Then, as number two seed, he had been beaten in the quarter-finals. He had returned in 1968 with open tennis, still a colossus of the courts, to make the finest recovery – and play the longest match ever seen at Wimbledon (112 games) – against Charlie Pasarell. Also to be remembered, Stan Smith, with the guardsman's ramrod back and Christian's nature; Jimmie Connors, who in 1974 had put paid in ruthless, barnstorming fashion to Ken Rosewall's last effort, but incredibly had succumbed the following year to an inspired game-plan by Arthur Ashe. Then we'd had Borg's marvellous run and his jousts with Connors and McEnroe. The 'IceBorg' had been an extraordinary exception. A record six times French Champion and almost certainly the greatest clay-court player ever, with his looping top-spin he had managed to adapt so successfully to Wimbledon's grass that his pre-dominantly baseline game had worn down all opposition. He had been a phenomenon – perhaps lucky not to have had to face great serve-volleyers before John McEnroe finally took his title from him. Lastly there had been McEnroe, that complete enigma – a hybrid of instinctive brilliant genius and sheer brat hooliganism.

As for the women, nearly every champion since the war had been capable of playing all-court tennis like a man – some more gracefully than others. The 1946 champion, Pauline Betz, played like a ballerina but still had a majestic game; Margaret Osborne (later du Pont) and Louise Brough, both superb players as friendly rivals and almost unbeatable together in doubles; Doris Hart, who somehow – though handicapped as a child by badly injured knee

5

tendons – mangaged to play a skilful and graceful game, while competing with the best of them; Maureen Connolly, 'Little Mo', with her bobbing head – in my mind the greatest woman player I have ever seen; Althea Gibson, the first black champion, who overcame so much difficulty and prejudice to get there.

Next in my memory that most majestic of champions, full of imperious power and graceful brilliance, Maria Bueno – for sheer eye-appeal she has been unsurpassed; that amazing athlete, Margaret Court – she should have been nicknamed 'All Court' – who won more Grand Slam titles than any other player (only terrible nerves at peak moments had kept her from being the greatest champion of them all); the ever-hungry, ever-chattering, fantastic fighter, Billie-Jean King; Britain's best postwar champion, lefthanded Ann Jones, with all Billie-Jean's determination and an awkward game to go with it – a game that could out-manoeuvre the best; that elegantly gliding Australian wood nymph, Evonne Goolagong, her onomatopoeic aboriginal name meaning 'tall trees by still waters' and her nature so often taking her 'walkabout' in the middle of a match.

Then came Centenary Year in 1977, with its wondrously timed win for Britain's unpredictable heroine, Virginia Wade (what a hallelujah day that had been!); and last but certainly not least those formidable foes, Chris Evert-Lloyd, the most consistent at a high level since Little Mo, and Martina Navratilova with her crushing all-powerful game. Theirs has been a long and thrilling rivalry – with business still to come.

And so I sit with my thoughts, my memories of past years. Years which – despite other commitments – have always been a new path to Wimbledon. Each year, as the opening day of the championships neared, my pulse has quickened in anticipation. And each year I have played a little game with myself, treasuring the time left as the rounds slip by, like a small boy with a box of sweets. First it would be one-twelfth gone, eleven left. After two days one-sixth gone, five left and so on, until the year's vintage was all too soon harvested. In 1982 a bonus was added. The championships were extended by one day, so that the Great God Television could have an even bigger feast – on the sabbath.

One of the service bands, which take it in turn each Wimbledon to play the audience in before the two singles finals, has been carrying me nostalgically back over the years. Now it's playing 'In the Mood'. Well, am I for this final act? Yes, very much so. I shall do my damnedest to make this my best Wimbledon performance ever, before the curtain for me irrevocably comes down. I could scarcely have hoped for a better theme, a more dramatic confrontation, than Becker versus Lendl.

But it's still only 12.30 – another hour and a half before 'curtain up'. I don't feel like going to lunch today – a small pork pie will do me (they're one of the better things from the modern catering in the press room – when you can get them). I'd rather sit and put out all my antennae and pick up every possible nuance adrift like dandelion puffs around the court.

I've seen so many great players and stupendous matches in this superb arena. I've often been asked what it's like to try to do a Wimbledon commentary. In answering I don't think I can do better than repeat what I wrote years ago:

> Doing a modern running commentary on a good singles match is like playing it yourself from both sides of the net. The constant effort of anticipating and giving as accurate a current description as possible, sustained over long periods of time at extremely fast speech speed, demands both mental and physical stamina. At the end of it the commentator feels the elation of the winner and very often the exhaustion of the loser.

Sometimes, to cope with a particularly fast and brilliant rally, I've felt a release of adrenalin flood into my brain, enabling me to keep pace and yet remain clear. At others, slips and spoonerisms have occurred. I remember in the fifties when the great Australians Hoad, Rosewall, Rose and Hartwig, certainly candidates for the best foursome ever, were playing such sparkling richocheting doubles that my tongue got completely twisted in trying to keep up, and I frequently called them 'Road' and 'Hosewall' and combined the two when referring to the Barnardo boys, who did the ballboying in those days, as 'Roseballs'.

Those slips resulted from trying to go fast, others occurred for various reasons. When in 1957 Christine Truman – soon to be sitting beside me to be one of the summarisers on the 1986 Men's Final – was making her famous charge as a sixteen-year-old and had reached the quarter-finals to play a good American, Betty Pratt, the whole of Britain was 'pulling' for her and I was extremely excited at the prospect of the match. Having done a preview while the players were hitting up, I ended it by saying, 'And now the umpire's called

7

"time" and they're getting ready for the fray – they're taking off their clothes!'

It was perhaps the same year that after the Ladies' Final, as the red carpet was swiftly being rolled out onto the court and the phalanx of ballboys was forming up, I suddenly realised with apprehension that I had forgotten to take the precaution of getting a feminine description of what the president of the club, the Duchess of Kent, was wearing. So as she came through the door below the Royal Box, I started circumspectly. 'Her Royal Highness', I said, 'is wearing a navy blue coat' – my mental geiger counter was operating furiously and gave me the 'all clear' on that – '. . . with a navy blue hat to match' – getting quite good, I thought – '. . . trimmed with white' – Robertson, you have a new career ahead of you! Emboldened, I sketched in my finishing touch '. . . and a row of three pearls'.

These 'disasters' were self-inflicted wounds, but sometimes events were beyond my control. In 1954, the final between Drobny and Rosewall was a climactic occasion. Drobny was the crowd's favourite – especially with the women. They also liked Ken Rosewall with his little-boy-lost look, but they felt that the youngster would certainly win the title before long whereas Drobny, they knew, had few chances left. It was a great match, which went to four sets. Rex Alston and I were doing commentary on alternate sets and so he had the finish. As the climax came I had been beside myself with excitement, and on the final point the crowd rose as one to give Drobny a standing ovation, the cheering lasting for what seemed like eternity.

After the umpire had given the score, Rex, sensing how much I wanted to express myself, turned to me saying, 'And now let's hear what Max Robertson thought about it.' I literally poured forth about ten minutes worth, the words feeling golden and I knew that I had done the best bit of reporting of my life. When I finished I felt the satisfaction of achievement and leant back contentedly. It was only later that I discovered that, as soon as the umpire had given the score, continuity had switched listeners to Lord's for the Varsity cricket match, and the engineers had not dared to tell me since I was in such exalted flight.

Drobny had been involved in another historic match the year before. Having failed to win in two Wimbledon finals, he must have felt that 1953 had to be his year, or his chances might vanish for ever. He was the number two seed but in the third round his way was barred by his great friend Budge Patty, the 1950 champion, who was seeded twelve. The match started at 5 o'clock and only finished in the late gloaming at 9.20. It proved to be the longest match to that date – ninety-three games in all.

Coming nearer the present, in 1983 I was commentating on a very boring and predictable doubles match between Fleming and McEnroe and the Gullikson twins, in which the twins were eventually easily beaten in straight sets. I have never been one who has been able to hide my feelings and – normally speaking – I believe that to be an advantage in a commentator, whose whole art is based on reaction to the events taking place before him. I believe this gives the commentator integrity and authority (as does admitting mistakes – provided it doesn't happen too often). If you tell the listener that the match is a poor one, when it is, he's much more likely to be carried with you when you say it's fantastic.

Anyway, on this occasion I had got thoroughly bored and turned to Christine Janes beside me, saying, 'This is really very poor stuff, Chris, don't you think? Who do McEnroe and Fleming play in the Final?' Christine and I have always enjoyed our game of badinage on the air, so she seized her chance, saying with some asperity, 'This *is* the Final, Max'.

My reverie is interrupted by the entry of Christine herself. She too wanted to get into the box in good time and has had an early lunch. However, she soon produces her usual bag of toffees while we chat in a desultory fashion. I tell her that I am trying to store up memories, so we play the game together and go into flashback.

Her presence makes me think of all the people who have worked with me in this box. To begin with after the war there was an immediate group comprising Rex Alston, Freddie Grisewood, Stewart MacPherson and Raymond Glendenning. Rex was in charge of Sports in Outside Broadcasts, but he also took part as a commentator at most events. He was an ex-schoolmaster and there was some pedagoguery in his manner which was exact and fairly dry, though laced sometimes with unexpected humour. Freddie was the old hand from pre-war, a county player himself with a marvellous charm in his very individual voice, so well known later to devotees of *Any Questions?*. Stewart was a Canadian and had made his name as an ice-hockey and boxing commentator and war correspondent. He knew little of tennis but his descriptions were always graphic and his transatlantic metaphors – some perhaps clichés in North America – seemed bright and fresh to British ears.

9

Finally there was Raymond who could do rapid commentary on any event and make it sound tremendously exciting and entertaining. He was known for his handlebar moustache and it seemed to add a bravura to his broadcasting which, though very colourful, was not always strictly accurate. This did not matter too much until the advent of television. Then, alas for Raymond, when actuality could be seen his flights of fancy were also apparent! But many listers didn't mind anyway and still found them diverting and enjoyable.

On the revival of television Freddie went to join them as their number one commentator and Stewart by now had gone back across the Atlantic. Rex, Raymond and I carried on together for a bit, sometimes helped in summary by Dan Maskell who in a year or two also went to television.

Fred Perry came into the radio team as a summariser in the very early days after the war. He has been a mainstay ever since. His authority as three-times-running champion and the last British one was a tremendous bonus to radio. His shrewd tactical comments came from the depth of his own experience in the days when he was dealing with such gamesmen as Jean Borotra. He was at his best perhaps when recalling his Davis Cup skirmishes with the French. Apart from commentary, for many years he and I also used to do an evening 'conversation piece' reviewing the day's play for overseas listeners. At times we had fierce arguments and he was not always right. From our countless hours of working together over such a long time we have become firm friends.

A completely different summariser was Alf Chave, whom I first met in Brisbane in 1938 at the State Championships of his beloved Queensland. He was then the established commentator – I the raw rookie – but he couldn't have been kinder to me, the no-nonsense kindness with which he also befriended many young players.

After that pre-war meeting I didn't see him again until 1956 when suddenly there he was, coming up over the horizon like the rising sun. He very quickly made himself part of our Wimbledon commentary team and was absolutely invaluable – as expert, friend and gen-prospector.

He had the ability to communicate vividly and succinctly his impressions and to draw relevant facts at will from a prodigious memory. But above all his value lay in his remarkable capacity to pick out the kernel of the situation at any stage of a match. Not only were his comments pithy and pointed but – without decrying genuine effort – he never pulled his punches. His timing was always superb and the aptness of his dictum was his own – Chavean.

One swallow doesn't make a summer but the first sight of Alf on his annual migration from Australia to Europe always awoke in me the anticipatory tingle of an approaching Wimbledon. So, when I first heard of his sudden death in August 1971, my very real regrets at the loss of the man were deepened by the knowledge that I would miss the herald.

Thinking of Alf reminds me of one of my most abiding personal memories of Wimbledon times – a memory not of tennis but of the cricket matches that used to be played between the Wimbledon press and the players on the middle Sunday of the championships. As the regular wicketkeeper/opening bat for the BBC I used to be one of the press stalwarts – and George Worthington, the captain of the players' side seemed to take a particular delight when my wicket fell.

George had been just under the top-class as a tennis player, twice getting as far as the fourth round at Wimbledon. When he gave up the world circuit he was promptly engaged by the All-England Club to be their coach, replacing Dan Maskell, who had become the L.T.A.'s Training Manager and also very involved with television. He was extremely popular, but never became softened by sojourn in England. Like any good Aussie he was tough and loved to win – especially when playing the Pommy press, against whom he invariably notched up a victory. He was often aided and abetted in this aim by his old pal from Queensland, Alf Chave, who always stood as one of the umpires. Indeed, there was one hilarious occasion when Alf, in urgent need, had retired from square-leg, without seeking permission, to attend to private business behind a bunch of nettles. As the bowler shouted an optimistic appeal from the wrong end, Alf happened to be stung at the moment critique in a sensitive part and a howl of 'Aoow!' nearly brought about the undoing of the batsman.

During one of these blood matches the somewhat inadequate bowling of the press was suffering at the hands of hawk-eyed tennis players. At the crisis Ray Lindwall, who had appeared late to perform for the press under the guise of a columnist in some daily paper (George Worthington had entered a protest which was not upheld), came on to bowl. Naturally, for the first over I stood back very respectfully. Obviously he was not bowling at anything like

Test speed – by club standards fast-medium. Feeling rather like a naughty boy, I asked him if he would mind me standing up? 'Naow', he replied, giving me an old-fashioned look.

The first ball was comparatively innocuous and the batsman managed to play it. The second, though, swung very late and moved off the wicket so much that the batsman, lunging out of his ground, got nowhere near it and I had to gather it at full extremity on the off-side, smartly whipping off the bails as I did so, with a triumphant 'Howzzat?' There was no question of the batsman being anything else than miles out of his ground, but there was quite a doubt as to the reaction of umpire Alf Chave, standing at square-leg. Sensing that Alf was winding himself up to support his Queensland colleague and say, 'Not aowt!', Lindwall marched threateningly towards him, with an extended accusing hand, and gave the emphatic order, 'Yew will give that aowt!' Even Alf could not ignore that.

On the fifth ball of the over Ray thought perhaps he would test me as much as the batsman. This time the movement on a perfect length was to leg. It was not so wide, thank goodness but, with the batsman missing and at the same time obscuring much of my vision, I did well to take it cleanly and whip off the bails again. 'Howzzat?' This time the margin of justice was much narrower but Alf's nerve had gone. He caved in and meekly put *one* finger up. Two stumpings in one over off Lindwall! He told me afterwards he had only ever had *one* in his life before. It was my most rewarding moment as a cricketer – almost worthy of Wisden!

If that was my best cricketing moment my best one in tennis came from the pen of Ray's partner in crime against England's batsmen, Keith Miller, who in Januaury 1974 wrote to me as follows:

My name is Keith Miller. I'm an Australian, and years back I used to play a bit of cricket for this country, tangling a few times with England.

That by the way. What this little note is for is simply this. Since I retired from cricket I've been writing cricket for your 'Daily Express' and I've spent the last eighteen Australian winters in the summer sunshine of England.

Naturally I've heard your tennis commentaries, and each time I hear you during Wimbledon, I always say to myself 'This man is such an outstanding commentator at Tennis I must write and tell him so and congratulate him'. So that's all this note is about. Simply to say how much I appreciate your work with the B.B.C.

Nothing else. Nothing sinister!! behind the letter. But thought in the Depth of your winter, when it appears that life is almost as grim as when I was flying on night fighters in the U.K. in second world war, this little air-letter from the sunny summer of Australia might warm your heart a little. I'll be listening again this summer.

I only met Ray Lindwall that once. I've never met Keith Miller. I sincerely hope that one day I will.

It was during the early days that most of the strange little incidents I remember occurred. I'll never forget when in 1949 the huge Dutchman, Hans van Swol, was playing the tiny Frenchman, Robert Abdessalam, in a second round match on the Centre Court. The Dutchman was near his last gasp in the final set when suddenly a squirrel ran onto the court and pertly took possession for some three minutes before being ejected, having unrepentantly bitten the ballboy who finally caught him. We were not on the air at the time and watching in the box with me were the Australian player, Jack Harper, and Ann Shead, another Aussie, for whom I worked regularly when she was producing *This Is Britain*, a magazine programme in the General Overseas Service – the forerunner of today's World Service. I yelled to the engineers to start recording and did a commentary, which is in the archives. Unfortunately, there was a noisy background of uncontrolled Australian laughter. That breather, however, had put new life into van Swol who then went on to win the match.

Thinking of van Swol reminds me of a Davis Cup doubles match he once played in at Edgbaston, also of course many years ago. He was partnered by Rinkl for the Netherlands and they were playing Tony Mottram and Geoff Paish. The ballboys fell far short of Wimbledon standards and the umpire – a brigadier of the old school – had reproved them on more than one occasion. In particular, a redhead doing duty at the net had transgressed more than once. Now, just as Mottram was swinging into his service action, this ballboy took it into his head to walk on court to retrieve a loose ball. We were on the air at the time, and in those days umpires were not so sophisticated in the ways of radio and television and did not automatically switch off their chair microphones for the sake of decorum – whenever there was any likelihood of altercation – the way they would today. I had paused for the score to be given, when to my utter astonishment I heard coming over the headphones (and therefore over the air) the umpire's voice ordering in the most venomous stage whisper, 'Get off, you redheaded little bastard!'

I smile a little at the memory, and focus my mind again on Wimbledon; what of the many other ghosts of the past? How many of their shades must be present in spirit today? For several years, when I first commentated from this box, I could look up to my right and see, sitting in the front row just behind the committee box, those venerable champions – the spark of their interest still fiercely alive – Mrs Lambert Chambers and Lottie Dod. They were both Wimbledon immortals, Mrs Lambert Chambers seven times a winner, Lottie Dod five times, and at fifteen, the youngest ever. I had interviewed them both and still have Mrs Lambert Chambers' handwritten account of her famous Challenge Round match with Suzanne Lenglen. And, of course, for a while after the war Queen Mary appeared regularly in the royal box, the epitome of dignity and majesty in her familiar toque hat.

Once open tennis had started in 1968 it was not long before radio coverage was vastly increased, with many more commentators and summarisers providing commentary and reports from a network of positions. The old amateur days had gone – in broadcasting as well as in tennis – and with them some of the fun. Now it is a huge operation and the listener is brilliantly provided for.

Bob Burrows became Head of Sport and Outside Broadcasts (Radio) in 1975 and, having an intense interest in sport and being particularly a follower of tennis, he masterminded and expanded the Wimbledon coverage and teamwork of today; and it was under him that the programme first ran daily without break from 2.00 – 7.00 pm. He was also a brilliant editor, instinctively knowing what was the key match situation that should be covered at any one moment. While he was at the helm new frontiers in coverage and technique were always being explored. Indeed, radio coverage of Wimbledon became so comprehensive, and so many viewers preferred to turn to it for commentary with their TV picture, that BBC Television was forced to look to its laurels and cast its net over more courts.

Bob was no respecter of persons, either. He used each man for what he was best at, regardless of what he might want to do.

Hitherto, I had nearly always done the interviews, coming down from the commentary box when word came through that a player was in the press interview room and should be available to us soon. This not only interrupted one's following of a match but meant that interviews were inclined to be rushed, especially as they were usually only allowed three minutes. Now, with plenty of time available in the expanded programme, they became a much more important ingredient. Gerry Williams, who had always been professionally involved in tennis, was brought in to do this and general rapportage and proved to be brilliant at it. I was sad not to do interviews any more but it made me available for whole-time commentary, and Bob paid me the compliment of using my talent to the full. I remember once in 1979 he moved me smartly from the Centre Court to number 2 where, in his fourth round match with Tom Gullikson, John McEnroe, the number two seed, was deep in the mire. I felt sorry for the man I was supplanting, but it was another instance of Bob using the forces at his command to the best of their capacities.

The main commentators to begin with under Burrows were Maurice Edelston, an Amateur Football international and commentator, Gerry Williams and me. A year or two later Maurice died suddenly, tragically early. Gerry and I had then carried on with the advent soon of Tony Adamson, a good player at junior level and a gifted broadcaster. The presenter of the programme from 1975, except when away on World Cup duty, was Peter Jones. Peter had been in charge of football at Radley College. Coming to the BBC as a football commentator, he had quickly made himself indispensable and nowadays turns his hand masterfully to practically any event in sport or ceremony. He is in a way a dinosaur, probably the last radio all-rounder in this era of specialisation.

Gerry Williams' talents were seized on by television in 1984 and Richard Evans, a globe-trotting tennis journalist with deep behind-the-scenes knowledge of the players and the increasingly complicated international tennis sphere, was brought into the main commentary body. Later still, David Mercer, an ex-solicitor and umpire of long experience, was taken onto staff contract, so that tennis rapportage would have more strength in depth. In the old days I was used on any tennis event that was being covered live with commentary. Since Gerry Williams had been appointed lawn tennis correspondent in 1976, I'd had less to do but was always used where much commentary was required, as for Davis and Wightman Cup

15

matches. With the much lamented departure of Bob Burrows to Thames Television, my role quickly decreased until soon Wimbledon had become my last refuge.

So my memories had been running on, bringing me ever nearer to the inexorable present that is now upon me. With a start I realise that it's 1.40 pm. The Centre Court is already nearly full and there is a hubbub of general anticipation, with everyone agog for what might be the tennis feast of the year. Our box is filling up. Christine is already beside me in the middle of the front row. On her left now is the second summariser, David Lloyd. With Tony presenting, Richard Evans is promoted to be my co-commentator on the Final and is sitting on the bench behind, ready to shift to my seat at the end of the first set. In the box next to us, with Tony Adamson, is that great doubles player, Frew McMillan, as incisive with his pithy comments as he had been with his two-handed volleys when partnering Bob Hewitt to three Wimbledon titles. Fred Perry, the greatest living name in British tennis is – with the other past men champions present – rightly ensconced in the Royal Box.

Rob Hastie, a delightful soft-spoken Scot, who is director for the first time this year, is calling us to check on our voice levels and give us last minute information and duties in the opening running order. At 1.52 pm there is a welcoming roar as the two gladiators come on court for the first all-European Mens' Final for ten years. Becker and Lendl turn in fair unison to bow to the Royal Box which is already full, with the president of the club, the Duke of Kent and his delightful Duchess, present for this great confrontation. Then the players turn back towards the umpire's chair and face the phalanx of clicking cameramen.

As the protagonists start their warm-up there comes into our headphones that blood-pulsing music especially written for – and which always opens – our programme and we're on our way. Tony Adamson welcomes listeners and we hear the prepared radio cocktail that sets up this match. Then, while the players are still hitting-up and having had a quick view from each of our experts, Tony introduces me with the words, 'And now we join Max Robertson for his last Wimbledon commentary'.

Last year, after seeing Becker win the Young Masters and then Queens, I had tipped him as a strong possibility for the title – incredible though that seemed at his age. This year pundits had all said it would be more difficult for him and, of course, in many ways

16

they were right. In 1985 his was a relatively untried lance tilting at the great ones. Now he'd become one of them and the others were athirst for his blood. But I still felt that he had that supreme champion's quality, instanced in the past consistently only by Maureen Connolly in my experience – the quality of instinctively raising one's game without flinch whenever a moment of peril arrives. Moreover, though Lendl, the great favourite of many for the title this year, was the world number one and had just won the French Championship for the second time, besides being the holder of the US title, my intuition told me that in his mind there must be a very strong question mark – with the rising tide of new young brilliance – as to whether he would ever win Wimbledon. And indeed it had been a very near thing for him in both his quarter-final against Tim Mayotte and his semi-final versus Slobadan Zivojinovic – both matches long five-setters. Even before that, in his fourth round match, he had been made to struggle by young Matt Anger, only winning 6/7 (7/9) 7/6 (7/2) 6/4 7/6 (12/10); though it could be said that the steel of his Wimbledon resolution, hitherto rather suspect, had been tempering in the fire of those battles. So it was that I had tipped Becker again – even before the tournament began.

Now I feel quite certain he is going to win and say so – perhaps the most telling reason being that this is Lendl's first final at Wimbledon, which he so badly wants to win, and Becker has been here before. To begin with Becker's not at his best, his all-powerful service not the accurate weapon we expected but, when in the middle of the first set he sees his coach's signal to throw the ball higher, he immediately gets into his stride. He wins the first two sets 6/4 6/3, but loses his first service game of the third set and is led 4/1. He breaks back to 4/4 but then Lendl, desperate for a set, plays an inspired six points to lead 5/4, and to bring Becker to 0/30 in the next game. At this point I say, 'I've said all along that when danger arises this boy goes for it. Let's see what's going to happen'. But Lendl wins the next point brilliantly and Becker is 0/40 – three set points to save.

I still feel utterly confident of Becker's character and also confident that he will raise his game. He does – with a vengeance – as a flood of adrenalin has him blanketing the net with an electrifying burst of fantastic volleys to reach deuce, then serving an ace for advantage and another colossal service to the backhand for the game. That finally breaks Lendl. At 30/30 on the Czech's service, Becker plays a superb top-spin backhand across court that lands on the line. He wins the next point to achieve the break, and holds his own service game for the match and his second title – still younger than any previous winner.

There is still Wimbledon business to come in the shape of the Mixed Doubles Final, but for me forty years and forty-one championships are over. My scorebook is closed for the last time.

2

A Pommy in Papua

M Y LAST WORKING LINK WITH THE BBC – WHICH HAS RULED SO MUCH OF MY LIFE – WAS SEVERED AS BORIS BECKER TOOK HIS second Wimbledon title. In many ways it was an apt conclusion, for Wimbledon has been the zenith of every year for me since the war, the warp of my BBC service; so perhaps it was fitting that it was there on the Centre Court that my service ended. It is also a good vantage point from which to look back over fifty years of broadcasting.

I began in May 1936 with a series of talks for the Australian Broadcasting Commission in Sydney, although nothing originally had been further from my mind than broadcasting in Australia. It was a man my parents had known in India who was, I suppose, indirectly responsible for the direction my life took.

I was born in Dacca, East Bengal, capital now of Bangladesh. It was a railway centre and my father was a *Burra Engineer Sahib* with the East Indian Railways. My paternal grandfather does not appear to have done anything very much. I believe he worked in the City for a while but retired early as a gentleman of private means – an euphemism that covered much at the time. In fact the means were so private that they were scarcely visible. Indeed, it was as a result of their almost reaching vanishing point, (even in those days of low income tax and micro-inflation) that my father had to leave Cheltenham College at the early age of sixteen. So, though he would have dearly loved to be a farmer, he became instead a railway engineering apprentice, starting on nine years of rigorous training at the Maidstone depot. Once qualified, he took up an appointment

19

in India where he met my mother, Renée Follit, who was nine years his junior.

My mother's family history was more exciting, the centre-piece being that through her mother, Flora, she was directly descended from Flora Macdonald. The story of her rescue of Bonnie Prince Charlie ('over the sea to Skye') and their night in a cave made a marvellous family saga for me and my sister Marian, who was nearly two years younger than me. The possibility of being descended from a royal by-blow lent pretension to pretence.

My maternal grandfather was an indigo planter in Bihar and then for some years secretary of the famous Calcutta Club, Tollygunge. I have only brief memories of him as a very charming and distinguished looking man, who was also rather deaf, the result we were told of taking quinine as a malaria preventative for most of his life.

Though I was born in India and did not leave permanently until I was five and a half, I don't remember much about it, but I still retain a vivid feeling of belonging in part and wanting to go back. I've only done so twice, both brief visits. The first time was to spend one night at Bombay airport on our flight to see the 1956 Olympic Games in Melbourne, when the heat and the crows by day and the mosquitoes, fireflies and starpricked velvet sky by night brought nostalgia flooding in. The second was for a fortnight in 1962 when I was contracted to be the guide and interviewer in a film of the World Ecumenical Conference in Delhi. On the way out our aircraft developed a fault and we spent a night again in Bombay. The hotel room and service left a lot wanting but I could look down on a scene that conjured up childhood at once. The street was teeming with the movement of a multitude of figures, eddying, swirling and side-stepping around inert sleepers and squatting beggars. And amid all this the slow-moving ox-drawn carts, the slightly faster *gharris* and the coolie-pulled rickshaws made their way – all to the accompaniment of yells, curses, adjurations or simply greetings.

A main ingredient of the film we had come to make, which had been scripted by that eminent journalist, James Cameron, was an inteview with the Archbishop of Canterbury, Dr. Ramsay. Cameron had written an opening in blank verse, which ran:

My Lord, how good to see you here,
So far from Canterbury.

The first time I said this it sounded faintly odd. However, as is the way with so many film directors, 'Take 1' is never right but quickly becomes 'Take 2', 'Take 3' and so on *ad nauseam*. The more I uttered these sententious lines, the more utterly ridiculous they began to sound – until suddenly both the Archbishop and I were laughing hysterically. The whole thing became impossible and we thankfully reverted to ordinary question and answer.

Other Indian memories are of little significance. However, although I have few childhood memories of India, I am sure that having been born overseas influenced my decision as a young man to leave England when I did – made me less wary of 'foreign parts'. So it happened that, in March 1935, when I was nineteen years old, I was preparing to sail on my first big adventure – prospecting for gold in Papua, New Guinea. A few days before leaving, I went to see a fortune-teller. She lived in Markham Square, just off the north side of the King's Road, Chelsea.

My mind was full of the coming voyage and what lay beyond it, and I was very excited. It had been quite a battle to convince my father that I should chuck up a Cambridge undergraduate's chances (after only one term's trial reading English) to seek the Pimpernel crock as one of a company of complete amateurs.

The reason I argued was that I thought I wanted to write and I knew that in order to do that, I would have to gain Experience of Life. Surely New Guinea would stand me in better stead than Cambridge? I did feel this quite sincerely but, if I were frank with myself, the deep underlying reason was that I had a terrible inferiority complex about the *cleverness* of the others in my English set and felt that, if I were to justify my father's considerable financial sacrifice in sending me to Cambridge, I would have to work very hard indeed – a prospect that did not please.

So it was that, feeling distinctly nervous, I rang the clairvoyant's front doorbell. I wasn't put exactly at my ease when I was ushered in by a maid into a very dark sitting room. The seer advanced on me. She was full-lipped, full-bosomed, black-eyed and black-haired. She was dressed darkly too, and wore a choker around her throat. Without preamble she asked, 'Do you want the five shilling or the ten shilling?' Seeing I was flummoxed, she said rather impatiently, 'It's five shillings to read your palm or ten shillings if I use the crystal'. I cautiously chose the five shilling fortune.

Without more ado she sat me down, took my hands, looked at them attentively for a few moments – and then told me that I would soon go on a long voyage. Good Lord! She followed with several more predictions that were more or less on the general target, but then she paused and looked rather puzzled. 'I can't quite make this out,' she said, and hesitated. 'I think you're going to make your living by your voice.' 'What!' I exclaimed in shock, 'I can't sing a note'. 'All the same,' she insisted, 'I feel sure you are going to use your voice a lot'. Looking back, I can't help wondering what she might not have told me for ten shillings. She did tell me that I was going to find something in clay and as it happened, the little gold we retrieved in Papua was washed out of a clay conglomerate. But still, it would have been nice to get everything 'crystal' clear.

Papua was certainly an experience, though I doubt that it taught me very much. We were a very mixed bag of amateurs, led in theory by an ex-Army colonel – the man (mentioned earlier) whom my parents had known in India. His son was working with a geologist prospecting for Guinea Gold, a company mainly interested in alluvial dredging. He had written to say that a small team should be able to pay its way, and if lucky, might strike it rich. This had been the basis of the New Guinea Gold Syndicate's prospectus and the final mix could well have been called 'The Likely Lads & Lassies'.

There were twelve shareholders, the colonel; his lady wife (who wore the trousers); their daughter; their old nanny; Fidlin, an ex-tea planter from Assam; Baird (an ex-IMMS colonel who had been on the Younghusband Expedition to Tibet in 1904; Hanrott (an ex-civil servant in South America); Mawson (ex-India, where my parents had known him also); Burt (a garage proprietor); Jackson (an engineer); Robertson (at the start the youngest); and finally Burgoyne (slightly younger than I, who had been working on my father's apple farm and whom I persuaded to join us), who came out a little later.

We went out in three parties. The advance party consisted of the colonel, Fidlin and Hanrott. The main party, made up of Baird, Burt, Mawson, Jackson and myself, followed about a month later. The rear party was composed of the ladies, the idea being that they would look after our base camp, grow vegetables and generally see to our domestic needs. When we arrived at Port Moresby we got word to follow the advance party to the old Lakekamu goldfield, which meant going a hundred miles up the coast in a small schooner called the *Ronald S*, ninety miles up the Lakekamu river in an old launch to Bulldog (a small airfield hacked out of the bush) and ten miles of footslogging through the jungle. The bush was the general Australian term for any forest – this being tropical rain forest of the densest kind. The 'walk' also involved crossing several rivers in spate by felled tree-trunks without any rails, or by crazy cane bridges. In our hobnailed boots we *Taubadas* (white men) teetered precariously across, our hearts in our mouths, while the barefooted porters carrying our baggage strolled across, even stopping and balancing on one foot to remove a leech or two.

Those leeches were a constant menace, for they loved the dripping conditions brought about by an annual rainfall of nearly 400 inches – we had a violent thunderstorm every afternoon. As you walked along, head down on the lookout for snakes, you could see the leeches' poor emaciated, starving little bodies, waving around on the track as they scented our approach (looking for all the world like miniscule elephants' trunks). Then they were on to you and busy at their noisome feeding. If you stopped to pick them off, more would hitch an unsuspected lift while you were engrossed. The only way to deal with them thoroughly was to wait until you got to camp and then have a thorough search, hoping they had not climbed further than your calves.

Sores also were a problem, especially since most of the food was tinned and lacking in certain essential vitamins. After a while even the slightest scratch would tend to fester. Another source of 'New Guinea sores' as they were called when they became really bad and began to eat into the bone, was the 'bush mocker', a red, crablike mite that bit and burrowed under your skin, setting up an intense irritation. If you scratched, which it was almost impossible to refrain from doing, you were likely to get a sore. We found that the best preventative for these ills was to anoint our whole bodies, after an evening's immersion in the river, with kerosene. This even helped to deter the nightly mosquito raiders.

But I have digressed. We arrived to find that a base camp had been set up and a sluice box or two were already being worked in the 'tailings' of the pre-World War I alluvial field. The advance party had been put onto this area by Viv Hides, one of a well-known pioneer family. The theory was that, by re-working the pre-war flats, the greatly increased price of gold (now A£8 an ounce) would allow us to pay our way while we prospected for better things.

But it soon became obvious, even to my innocent eyes, that we were a hopelessly top-heavy party. The accepted proportion of working Papuans, 'boys' as they were called, indentured for eighteen months at a time as paid labour, to 'white' men was twenty to one – that is if any sort of economic proposition was to be carried out with a hope of success. We were twelve in theory and we had a work force of only forty. Freight, either by the same route we had travelled, or for urgent supplies by air to Bulldog, was expensive and we were certainly not paying our way. The rear party was soon due and the failure he would have to confess was preying on the colonel's mind. He was a nice, gentle person – saving his one passion of big game shooting. The only game in Papua, however, apart from alligators, were wild pig, wallaby and the occasional cassowary – an emu-like bird.

One morning, just before dawn, when the jungle birds' chorus was at its loudest, a single shot stilled them for a moment. The poor colonel had killed himself. It was the first time death had been personal to me, though the others were very good and didn't let me see the corpse. Instead I was put to busying myself by helping Burt to construct a simple wooden coffin.

We all admired the colonel's lady, who insisted on her party finishing the journey. This they did, carried for some distance on litters. A sad final winding-up meeting of the 'New Guinea Gold Syndicate' was held, only three months after the main party had arrived. It was decided that Fidlin should henceforth be the leader and he, Burgoyne (who had recently arrived) and I bought the assets and carried on for six months. But, though we were now just paying our way, it was not a proposition to entertain for long. We were steadily becoming more unhealthy as the imbalance of vitamins told. At one point, due to a mistake in our stores order by the universal suppliers in that area, Burns Philp (known not so affectionately as the Bloody Pirates), we had nothing to eat for six weeks but tinned herring, crab or sardines. Herring and crab I have been unable to face ever since.

I had also had a pretty bad go of malaria, so I reckoned it was time to give Papua best and get out while the going was good. I felt rather a renegade, leaving Fidlin and Burgoyne in the lurch, but they, too, packed it in only a month or so later.

Fidlin I met again once after the war when I was working at some exhibition. He looked just the same, still with the 'Navy Cut' beard he had sported in the New Guinea jungle. Burgoyne, alas, was killed in the war. Mawson, Burt and Hanrott returned home and I heard no more of them. Jackson, who turned out the best of us as an 'operator', and had moved on to another company, had one lucky strike and became something of an entrepeneur, I believe. I saw him once in England many years ago. Finally, Colonel Baird, who was sixty-five at the time, went back to Australia, married the tall leggy brunette (some thirty years his junior) he had met on the outward voyage and settled in Norfolk Island, where he became Chief Magistrate, raised a new family and was very respected.

My most endearing memory of Papua was seeing Doc Baird, who had had plenty of experience in dealing with army malingerers, taking our 'boys' sick parade. There were one or two regular triers-on but the doctor had a way with them. Mapu was a big fellow, with bubo and sore scars aplenty. When he wanted a day off working a box, he appeared, grimacing as if in great pain. Pointing to an old bubo scar that he had deliberately inflamed, he said, 'Him big hurt, Taubada'. 'Is it?', said the doctor, thoughtfully picking up a large bushknife (as used for hacking out a track) and testing its keenness with his thumb. 'Yes, I can see you're in pain, Mapu. I think we'd better cut it out.' As the knife came nearer Mapu experienced a sudden and miraculous cure. Then there was Wassai, a little runt but a trouble-maker. He would be holding his stomach and looking fit to die. 'Me got heap big tummy trouble, Taubada.' 'All right Wassai', said the Doc, 'I give you big murra-murra (medicine). You heap better bimeby', whereupon he ladled out a goodish dose of castor oil, adding a pink cough tincture for good effect. It was just as well to make certain. The next in line was Wogai, holding his head and looking very pained. 'Head him hurt big', moaned Wogai. He got much the same big murra-murra as Wassai. They were both told to come back for more in four hours, if they weren't better. They seldom did.

The other memory is of a small adventure I had. Fidlin and I were on a prospecting trip and, having set up camp in the upper reaches of the Cassowary, we had put in one or two experimental boxes to see whether it was worth trying a bigger operation. One evening, having returned to camp and looking forward to a refreshing bath and then kai-kai (food), we found an anxious-looking deputation of the 'boys' waiting for us. 'Big snake, Taubada,' they said, pointing to the other side of the river along a new track we had made. Judging by their rolling eyes and wide fisherman-like gestures with their hands, it was indeed a big snake. If so, it could only be a reticulated python.

'You'd better go and see what it is,' said a disinterested Fidlin. I was just leaving, with nothing but the 45 ex-service revolver we all carried but were hopeless shots with, when Fidlin said, 'I'd take your shotgun, if I were you'. So I did and our 'fearless explorer, followed by his faithful men, went warily up the track, imagining a huge python barring his path at any moment, or dropping out of a tree to coil itself round him and squeeze and squeeze. . .' Eventually the boys signalled to me to slow down – not that I was going fast – and there suddenly it was. It did indeed bar the track but luckily it must have recently had a large meal, for it was fast asleep and showed no sign of being aware of us.

But I wasn't taking any chances. It was gigantic. Its coils seemed to go on for ever and its body was thick, quite thick enough, I felt, to engorge a man. Its head was lying on top, facing away from me, I was glad to see. All this 'the great white hunter appraised in a flash of his derring eye – but what was he to do? If he backed off, saying "let the poor brute digest its meal in peace", he would for ever lose face. There was only one course open to him. On tiptoe he edged towards the vast reptile, his gun extended before him. Would its animal sixth sense awaken it in time to take mortal action? At last he reached it. It still did not stir. . . '

With the utmost caution I pointed the tip of the barrel at the nape of its thick neck, holding it only an inch or two away. For a millisecond that seemed an eternity I held my breath . . . and then fired both barrels. The result was highly dramatic. Death must have been instantaneous, but the python still managed one convulsive death-throe bound into the air – fortunately away from me – and crashed down the hill beside the track. It was quite dead and measured just under twenty-five feet (the record length for this species being over 30 feet). I was trembling with reaction, but did my best to look nonchalant. I was not sure whether I went up or down in the boys' estimation for this action – 'a deed that no true sportsman would have contemplated'.

Looking back on it in cold hindsight, rather than sweat, I realised how ridiculous I must have looked as I stalked the sleeping giant. The python certainly had the last laugh, for it was far too big and unwieldy to lug away through the undergrowth. Nor would it burn successfully. Each day we all had to pass the spot on our way to the boxes and each day the stench got worse. It seemed to be rubbing the ridicule in. Fidlin said nothing as he averted his face but his look spoke volumes. I got the distinct feeling he would have managed the affair rather better.

I had originally been given the job of making that track along the top of a narrow ridge. One of the boys, a deaf-and-dumb named Kwakurra, was ahead of me doing the initial cutting. I was immediately behind him, checking with my compass that he was keeping more or less on the right bearing. Behind me were two other boys, who were widening and clearing the track properly. Progress was slow but steady, when suddenly Kwakurra turned upon me, his knife raised above his head, his mouth open in a ferocious expression. Thinking he was suddenly running amok, I threw myself sideways and rolled down the hill getting many a gash from 'wait-a-while' thorn in the process. Instead of pursuing me Kwakurra charged back up the track, taking the others with him. He had unwittingly hacked into a wild bees' nest and their fury had turned on him.

Those bees could be an awful nuisance. Usually they were tiny and an individual sting or two were of little consequence, but anyone mauled by a whole colony would know all about it.

Funnily enough, though we often felt they were around and certainly keeping good tabs on us, I never saw any Kukukukus, the generic name for the local tribes inhabiting the foothills of Mount Lawson. We had heard a lot about them, for it was only recently that they had been cured — some said not entirely — of their fond habit of headhunting and sometimes cannibalism. In this connection their gastronomic sounding name was rather suggestive. At any rate, they never bothered us. Perhaps we were too easy game.

Quite early on, as I came to realise that Papua did not promise much for me, I cast around for ways to salvage something from my experience. I was corresponding with Nancy Suttor, a Sydney girl, whom I'd met on the voyage out to Australia, and asked her to buy me a 16 mm cine camera. This she managed to do, a secondhand Kodak for £12. It was a splendid camera — I only wish I had it now. Having read the instructions carefully, I loaded it and filmed the departure of the colonel's lady and her retinue. I felt I had got some very good shots of them being transported across the Cassowary in litters; but, alas, it transpired that I had loaded the film back to front. After that disaster I did manage to get it right and in the end produced an amateur silent film of box-sluicing for gold, with the written captions that were used in those days. I sold one copy to the Department of Education in New South Wales and there's now one in the BBC's television archives.

My father put another thought into my head, when he wrote to the BBC suggesting that I might take part in the round the world Christmas Day Programme, linking the countries of the Empire, which was such a feature of broadcasting in those days. What possessed him I can't think, and he got a bland but dusty answer and yet from that thought my future 'prospects' were to grow.

3

I Take to the Air

BACK IN SYDNEY, THINKING THAT IT WAS ONLY A STAGING POST ON MY WAY HOME TO ENGLAND, I WENT TO SEE THE AUSTRALIAN Broadcasting Commision's Head of Talks, who turned out to be a Mrs Gladys Moore. She was very kind to me and influenced my career considerably. She readily agreed to me doing five talks on my New Guinea experiences under the series title of 'A Pommy In Papua'. The pay was a magnificent one and a half guineas per talk. This meant that at least the lodgings I had found near the Suttors in Darling Point Road, one of Sydney's best residential areas, were taken care of for five weeks.

During the first talk, my first ever broadcast, I had an extra-ordinary experience. Mrs Moore brought me up to the studio of Station 2FC, and introduced me to the announcer at his desk. She settled me down at a speaker's table in the middle of the studio and, after the engineer (whom I could see through a glass panel in the control cubicle) had taken my voice level, she left me to listen in the cubicle. At the appointed hour the announcer announced me and my subject and, as a red light came up on my table, he signalled me to start.

I did so and was reading quite happily from my script when I noticed him quietly get up and leave the studio. I began to feel very strange. What was I doing here, sitting alone in the middle of a large room and talking to myself? I felt odder and odder and gradually became aware that I was no longer in my body but floating near a corner of the ceiling, looking down from sideways and slightly behind at this ridiculous creature sitting there talking to no one. So ludicrously nonsensical did the situation seem that my watching mind very nearly exerted enough influence on the moronic one still in my body to stop me talking. How long I remained up there, outside myself, I really couldn't say, but it was touch and go whether I stopped talking or not. Back in myself, still very much aware of the absurdity of it all, I just managed to keep going till the end, the sense of unreality getting stronger all the time. I have often heard since of people having this kind of experience but thank goodness it has never happened to me again.

Mrs Moore seemed pleased with the talks and suggested that I should take an announcer's test. I did it and it was pronounced promising. The idea of becoming an announcer began to appeal strongly, especially since I was seeing more and more of Nancy. Besides, I told myself, wouldn't it be much better to make out on my own with a job here than trail home confessing failure? Thanks to running away from Cambridge, I had no qualifications and, though unemployment was nothing like as bad as it is today, jobs were not easy to come by at that time in England. But, although I attended several auditions, no announcer's job materialised.

Money was becoming a problem, although for a while I had a job with a tea and coffee broker, trying to sell to cafes and restaurants. I had scant success. Then I was offered a living-in job at a small junior grammar school at Killara, a Sydney suburb on the North Shore line. I was there for a term. I quite enjoyed it but realised that I was not really cut out for it either, since being serious by nature I was too easily ragged. It was now nine months since I had got back to Sydney. Just as I was becoming desperate, fate intervened and I received two offers of announcer's jobs on the same day. The first was to join the ABC in Sydney at £5 a week, the second to go to a commercial station in Brisbane, at £6 a week. Sydney won because I felt the ABC's prestige was higher and I also wanted to be near Nancy.

The experience I gained with the ABC was ideal for my postwar work with the BBC. As an announcer you seldom had any script to read – except the News. By day you were playing what seemed to be an endless succession of discs, with the occasional speaker or small musical ensemble to break the monotony. Everything, except outside broadcasts (which in those days were nearly always sport or orchestral and celebrity broadcasts from the Sydney Town Hall) took place in the one studio.

Announcers were kept pretty busy. Logging all the details of the discs played for royalty payments took most of the time they were playing. Getting the needle into the right groove was quite an art. You rested the point of the needle on the middle finger of your hand, so that you could guide it onto the record as you finished announcing and before fading it up. Works that lasted longer than one side were the most difficult – especially for someone as unmusical as I. It was so easy to cross-fade into the other and find that some of the notes were being played twice over. A perfect fade over, whether by chance or not, gave a happy sense of achievement (job satisfaction it would be called in today's jargon). The constant repetition of this 'guiding' technique for playing records produced a thick callous on my middle fingers, rather as a squash racket handle will on the inside of the thumb.

We were regarded as the programmes' hosts and for the evening session, which began at 6.00 pm, we always wore a dinner jacket. We received speakers and tried to put them at their ease. Mindful of my own experience, if I got a first-timer or someone clearly nervous, I always stayed in the studio and was as attentive as possible to what was being said. You soon got to know the professionals and the members of the small ensembles who played for us. One small group was particularly fond of playing gypsy music. Still as unmusical as ever, and perhaps concentrating on writing up my log, it was very easy, when a Czardas or something similar was being played, to announce the next piece before the last was finished. Having done this a couple of times the leader and I agreed that I would wait for his nod.

When records were announced we were required by an agreement with the record companies to mention four points each time – the names of the artist, the piece, the composer and the recording company. I didn't want to get into a repeating groove myself, so I varied the order and way of putting those four facts as much as possible. Unconsciously I was learning to ad lib and to feel at ease with the microphone.

When I joined the ABC it had one ace in its pack that the commerical stations found it impossible to trump. His name was Watts (Denis Watts, I believe) but to the whole of Australia he was known simply as 'Watto'. He was a cheery, genial, wise-cracking, sophisticated man in the Ben Travers mould, who ran the Early Morning Session and had the whole of Australia by the ear. The horrible business of getting up and having a hurried breakfast was lightened by listening to Watto, who made life seem a joke or a song. At the time he was quite unique in his approach and the commercial stations gnashed their teeth as they vainly tried to match him and give their advertisers something to buy. But Watto was wont to burn the candle at both ends and one Saturday morning he paid the price. He had a stroke in the middle of making one of his inimitable cracks and died that afternoon. The country went into mourning.

On the basis that nobody could replace Watto, I suppose our bosses felt that something quite different was called for – perhaps the callow youth of Robertson. So they gave me the job and for three months I strove to fill the aching void. Recently I found some of my old scripts and, judging by them, the commercial stations must have had a field day. But I found one great ally, a dear soul called Minnie Hutchens, who was probably my only fan and used to write regularly to me, enclosing jokes and other snippets cut out of the papers. I never met her but she was invaluable. Without her contributions and her boost to my morale I would have found it very hard to carry on.

Apart from studio work I was doing a fair number of outside broadcasts for, provided you did not ask for more money, the station manager would let you do pretty well anything you liked, if you showed any aptitude for it. My first tennis commentary was on a semi-final of the 1937 Australian Championships between that majestic Wimbledon champion of 1932, Jack Crawford and Vivian McGrath, the first player with a great doublehanded backhand. McGrath won and went on to beat John Bromwich in the final, a match I also described. I was also occasionally taking part in radio plays and even, under the friendly tutelage of Edmund Barclay (the Commission's staff scriptwriter) adapting some of Henry Lawson's short stories for radio. It was a comprehensive experience I was gathering and it proved invaluable.

Nancy and I were now 'going strong' as they used to say. She was a lovely girl, with beautiful piercing blue eyes and a noble brow behind which was a very good brain. In the autumn of 1937 she said one day, 'They're advertising for young men to train as pilots for the Citizens' Airforce [the equivalent of Britain's "Volunteer Reserve"]. Why don't you apply?' There was a challenging 'prove yourself, if you're really interested in me' nuance in her tone. So I thought about it and the more I did, the more the idea appealed for other reasons. It seemed pretty obvious that a war was coming. There had not been a *blitzkrieg* yet and people still thought about war as stagnation in lines of trenches. Having, as a result of schoolday ragging, always found it difficult to perform my private functions with anyone around, I rather took to the idea of operating from behind the lines in proper billets.

Not perhaps the best of reasons to prompt a pilot's application. I had never itched to fly as many boys do, but I liked driving a car and I had a good eye for ball-games, both needing good reflexes. So why not? I applied and to my surprise was accepted. This meant a three-month secondment from the ABC to attend the course at Richmond Airfield, the RAAF aerodrome about twenty miles from Sydney. I was sorry to be parted from Nancy, though I would be able to get back at most weekends, but it was with quite a sigh of relief that I handed over the Early Morning Session. Apart from anything else, I had been burning the candle at both ends, too.

There were about ten cadets on the course, all Australians except for me and one of the Governor's ADCs, Blake Pelly, who was thirty. I was just twenty-two, very inexperienced in life and love (I thought literally that if you wanted to kiss a girl, you wanted to marry her) and rather a shy loner by nature. Perhaps sensing my difficulties the CO took me as his pupil. I got on very well with him. To begin with I found he shouted at me when I did something wrong. When I told him not to because it put me off, he took it like a lamb, perhaps out of sheer surprise. Under his instruction I progressed quite well. I had the natural games player's judgment of speed and distance and I was gradually gaining confidence.

Perhaps because I was the CO's pupil, I was the first to go solo, after seven and a quarter hours' of dual tuition. All seemed to be going reasonably well, though two aspects of my training did bother me. The first was the technical side of things. I could usually understand the principles at the time, if they were clearly and patiently explained but, because engineering was really foreign to my nature, I could never hold the knowledge. I realised – and so I think did the instructors – that I would never have that intimacy with the capacities of the machine that I was flying, that might be invaluable in an emergency. The other worry was the feeling of not fitting in with the Aussies when we were off duty.

Soon after I had gone solo the CO was posted away and I think that sealed my fate. Thereafter I had a succession of instructors when somebody had a spare period. There was no one to take a consistent interest in me, and of course, all instructors have individual approaches to the job. My confidence was deteriorating.

It was not helped by having a couple of forced landings, both of which temporarily wrote off the aircraft. As there were only three, I was not popular.

The first forced landing was brought about by my 'losing my prop' when practising a flick turn. If I had remembered a lecture we had had, I could have corrected by diving – as Biggles would certainly have done (he, of course, would not have lost it in the first place) – and the increasing speed would have started the propeller turning and caused the engine to fire. Instead I looked hastily for a field. Ah, there was a nice big one conveniently below me! It had a lot of objects scattered around on it, which I took to be grazing cattle. Surely they would get out of the way if they saw me coming? Anyway, there was no other field of the right size nearby.

I turned away to lose height and get into the right approach path. By the time I could see the field again, I was down to 500 feet. Now, I saw that the objects were not cattle but large jagged tree-stumps. It was far too late to try for another field. I could see one clear but narrow lane that gave me hope. Could I make it? I knew it would be a near thing, for a slight cross-wind was causing me to drift away to the right. As I neared the ground, I realised I'd misjudged it. At least I made a reasonable landing and she went rolling on. I was now powerless to do anything except hold her straight and pray, for the aircraft's nose-up attitude prevented me from seeing anything directly in front of me.

Expecting a horrible crash at any second, we seemed to run on for an eternity, gradually losing momentum. When it came I was lucky, for we hit with a wing-tip and not head-on. Fortunately she had lost enough way not to flip over but came to rest, having described a half-circle round the tree-stump. Suddenly there was stillness and silence except for the sinister sound of dripping . . . petrol! I was out of my straps and the cockpit in very quick time. Needless to say, when he arrived with the recovery truck, the 'chief' in charge of maintenance made it very clear that I was not his favourite son.

That little incident had scarcely been forgiven – if not forgotten – when the second happened. I'd been told to go up and practise forced landing approaches to the two or three fields in the aerodrome's circumference that were designated as the easiest, if engine failure (most common just after take-off) should occur. I'd already experimented satisfactorily with two of the fields and perhaps this had given me a little fatal over-confidence. Taking off from the aerodrome and gaining a little height I shut off the throttle and started a glide approach to the third field. All was going well and I was about to open up the engine and depart when I suddenly noticed to my horror some telephone wires just ahead of me.

Again Biggles would never have allowed this situation to develop but if he had he'd have known an immediate remedy. My reaction was to do what is instinctive to any inexperienced pilot. I shoved open the throttle and pulled on the joystick to bring the plane's nose up. This gave me the false feeling that I was clearing the obstacle, whereas what I was in effect doing was cutting down speed and asking for a stall. I got it – just as we staggered over the wires. The next thing I knew was that we were on the ground, having pancaked from a great height. I switched off hastily and again there was the unforgettable sound of dripping petrol. I abandoned ship fast. This time the chiefie's reaction was totally unprintable. Robertson was in the doghouse with a vengeance.

Against this unfortunate background, the end of the course was approaching with most of the cadets unable to get their 'wings' in time, since the training schedules had been so badly interrupted by my not so 'wizard prangs'. Before the second I had learned the rudiments of formation flying, which I rather enjoyed, and some simple aerobatics like stall turns, flick turns and looping the loop. Early in our training we were shown how to get out of a spin before it got out of hand and also sideslipping to lose height quickly. I remember once innocently sideslipping in over the airfield boundary and, straightening at the critical moment, I found I had landed virtually without any forward movement. I was lucky not to be seen, for this was strictly forbidden as a tiny miscalculation or freak gust of wind could bring disaster.

The manoeuvre that was my undoing was the 'slow roll', which is a corkscrew movement that turns the aircraft vertically through 360 degrees on its flying axis. When my instructor did it for me, I fell out in my shoulder straps as we turned over and my feet came off the rudder-bar. When he asked me to do it with his guidance, the same thing happened and I knew that I'd played no part in it. Sadly, I did not have the moral courage to tell him so. When he told me to go up solo and do it, I knew I couldn't. The nearest thing in my experience to it was trying to turn a somersault under water and being completely disorientated before buoyancy brought me to the surface.

Time and time again I tried and got further and further onto my side . . . but I could not make myself go completely over, for I knew with utter certainty that if I did I would never come upright again. I think that was the real breaking point. If only I'd had the courage to tell, if only the CO had not been posted. My failure in the air led me more and more to brood and keep to myself in the mess, so I had no one to talk the problem out with. As I left at the end of the course I had to admit to myself that I now dreaded having to do aerobatics. My nerve had gone.

As soon as I got back to the ABC I was asked by the General Manager if I would go up to Brisbane, as School Broadcasts officer for Queensland, combined with announcing and commentating. I longed to say 'Yes', for it was promotion, but I felt it would really be running away from my flying problem, as I knew there were no training facilities up there. So I declined politely and knew at once from the GM's face that he was disappointed in me and that I had probably earned a black mark on my record.

As luck would have it, the man appointed in my place suddenly fell ill and I let it be known that I had realised my mistake and, if I were given a second chance, would gladly accept. I was and now I was committed. I had talked things over with Nancy and we had agreed that if I got the Brisbane job, which meant a little more pay, we would get married. The appointment was immediate, so I went on up to Brisbane, Nancy following a month or so later and we were married in May 1938. I was twenty-two, she was twenty-five and life seemed wonderful.

I was enjoying the variety in my work. My boss, Huck Finlay, was a lovely man. He had been a rugby international, touring Britain with the 'Waratahs'. He gave me my head and his backing and, in the eight months I had under him, I developed as a broadcaster. In commentary I did tennis, cricket, rugby (I shared commentary with him on an international between Australia and the All Blacks) and rugby league. As to School Broadcasts, what the Education Committee (average age about seventy) thought of this young Pommy I dread to think but, whether Huck had asked them to be forbearing or whether it was their natural kindliness, they were very co-operative.

But there was still the problem of flying that clouded my horizon, and it came to a head one morning horribly and dramatically. I got in late to read the news, so did not have time to glance through and rehearse it to myself before I was on the air. The very first item stopped me in my tracks and it was all I could do to start again and finish the news. It reported the crash from 20,000 feet on his first height test of the cadet who had been the best of our bunch.

I was completely devastated and knew that I was finished. This happened to coincide with a time when I was already making up my mind to take the plunge, leave ABC and try my luck with the BBC at home. Although I liked Australia and the Aussies, I felt I did not want to settle there but I knew that, given another year or two, I might feel differently. To this end, while I had still been in Sydney the previous autumn, I had made a disc recording with Colombia (it cost me ten guineas), showing my paces as an announcer. I knew Gladys Moore was going on a world trip that would include an official visit to the BBC and I asked her if she would take the disc. This she gladly did and, though the reply that eventually came back from the director of Empire Programmes promised nothing, it did say that if I came they would be pleased to see me. Looking at the evidence I felt I had received a sort of 'dare' invitation. If I failed to accept the challenge I was likely to regret it always.

I managed to get an interview with my new CO, who was up in Brisbane for an enquiry, and explained the position. Though I'm sure he saw through me, he was very nice and gave me my discharge. I had, of course, discussed it first with Nancy, and somewhat to my surprise she liked the idea. Perhaps this was because she had really enjoyed her trip 'home', as most Aussies used to call Britain. And so the decision was made.

4

THE END OF AN ERA

SO OFF WE WENT IN JANUARY 1939. HUCK GAVE ME HIS BLESSING. I
DON'T THINK THE GM REALLY APPROVED THAT I WAS LEAVING SO
soon after I had accepted his second chance, but he was mag-
nanimous enough to give me a sort of *laisser-passer* letter to present
to any broadcasting authority, for Nancy and I had decided to have
a delayed honeymoon by getting off the ship at Naples and
wending our way back to England overland by train. In Naples we
lingered a few days like any tourists, fascinated by our visit to
Pompei.

But soon we moved on to Rome. Blackshirted Fascism was rife
everywhere. As luck would have it we had arrived just in time for
the Coronation of Pope Pius XII. I cabled the ABC, who said they
would be delighted to have a piece from me. But, not being a
Catholic, could I get in? I presented my *laisser-passer* letter at RAI,
(the Italian broadcasting service) and got an observer's pass without
difficulty.

The day dawned and I was afoot early – so it seemed was the
whole of Rome. And the whole of Rome seemed to be inside St
Peters! I had never been there before and was amazed at what I saw.
The interior was almost like a fairground, where different groups in
different garbs all talked and gesticulated together. My pass took
me halfway up the central aisle and I stood on the right facing the
altar. On all sides were a mass of people and all of them seemed to
have brought picnic lunches, some even having stools. (One fat
prelate fell off his and his picnic was scattered on the floor – to vast
amusement.) How wise they were, because it was a long time

before the door from the Cistine Chapel opened and the Pope was borne in by the *Sediari*, the chair-bearers, in formal procession.

But there was nothing formal about the throngs in the aisles. His progress was heralded first down the southern side aisle, a swelling roar of '*Papa – Viva il Papa!*' with storms of applause being repeated over and over again. It was a moving and majestic and yet very human occasion as the Pope was borne round the cathedral and finally up to the high altar, bestowing his blessing from side to side.

By the greatest of good fortune I found myself standing next to a young priest – an English novitiate – who was attending the German College just on the north side of the cathedral. His name was Peter Venables. It was through him that I met Harmon Grisewood – a BBC planner and also a leading Catholic, who was in Rome to do the commentary on the coronation.

After the ceremonial and excitement was over, Peter and I drifted away with the crowds and found our way to a restaurant, where Peter had arranged to meet Harmon and his Vatican mentor, a most urbane cleric who was our host. It was a lovely spring day and we ate in the open, enjoying a leisurely and most civilised meal. The ambience was perfect and it would have been difficult not to strike up a rapport. Harmon was a delightful person, and we got on very well in those expansive circumstances. He was one of the two planners whose job it was to schedule all BBC programmes. He was a true scholar and a well-rounded person, absolutely suitable to carry out the BBC's function of 'to inform, instruct and entertain'. He was genuinely interested in my pilgrimage and said, 'When you get to London, come and see me and I'll do what I can to help'.

With lightened heart and full of optimism at having found an important ally, I joined Nancy in seeing as much of Rome as possible. Time was short. Mussolini's troops started the rape of Albania while we were there. His voice could be constantly heard on the radio, ranting and adjuring with bombastic appeals to patriotism. We even saw him once appearing on the balcony of his palace in the Piazza Venezia, while a parade goose-stepped below. It was time to move on. We spent some magical spring days in Paris and then in May came the welcome sight of the white cliffs of Dover, which we had last seen four years before.

I lost no time in ringing Harmon Grisewood, and to my delighted surprise I was put through at once. It was only later that I discovered I owed this to there already being a Max Robertson in the BBC's music department. The gods were truly on my side. I only met my namesake once, for he was killed in the war.

Harmon was very helpful. He had obviously done some lobbying on my behalf. I also went to see Mr McGregor, director of Empire Programmes to whom Gladys Moore had taken my disc. The result of these combined efforts was that I was asked to attend an audition. By sheer chance I was making my effort at a very good moment, for the BBC needed some fresh announcers for the European Service, which would shortly be starting. No one realised then quite how vital that new service would become. It was to be listened to in more hope, despair, animation, secrecy and, above all, respect than any other broadcasting service has ever been, or is ever likely to be again.

Soon I received the incredible but infinitely exhilarating news that I had been chosen and was to report for duty in mid-May, when I found two other 'new boys' starting with me. When we three newcomers, Gibson Parker, (a Northern Irishman with a soft lilting voice and much charm), Tony Beamish, (who had an exaggerated drawl like many public school educated lads of the day) and I (who had also been one of those but, with my voice perhaps lightened by its Australian experience) first started in the European Service, our senior hand was Bob Dougall (of later TV news-reading fame), who had been a while with the Empire Service. I think we all of us – certainly I did – thought ourselves most important when we opened up a programme and said 'This is London calling . . . *Ici Londres* . . . *Hier ist London* . . . *Parla Londra*'. In my case the vocabulary did not go much further, although Gibson and Tony were pretty good at French and the latter was also a good German speaker. Bob Dougall had an insouciant charm and was not the best of timekeepers when taking over for his own spell of duty – the prerogative, he no doubt thought, of seniority.

But first came our 'training' with the Home announcers in the national and regional programmes. In the excitement of starting a new job with such an important concern as the BBC – if not the voice of Reith any longer it certainly seemed still to be the voice of the deity – life appeared enlarged and heightened. It gave one a tremendous godlike sense of privilege to belong to it and I'll never forget how my puffed up pride was pricked on the very first day when, coming out of Broadcasting House to go down to Oxford Street tube station, I crossed over to the All Souls', Langham Place

pavement where two boys were playing in the gutter. One looked
up and demanded cheekily, 'autograph mister?'. In lordly fashion I
obliged. However, I got my come-uppence immediately for, when
I turned around a few yards later, I observed the two boys looking
at my mame in puzzlement before tearing it up with disgust!

Our 'training' was in the hands of a man called Commander
Kingbull whom we sometimes felt to be aptly named. We were
being taught to read the news impartially and precisely, without the
slightest personal inflection, ev e ry syll ab le weigh ing
eq ual ly. The nearest one might come to expression was to allow a
sombre tone in one's voice when giving news of a death or disaster.
The most solemn item I remember having to announce to the
nation was the loss of the submarine *Thetis*, which in the summer of
1939 shook everyone as a profound tragedy. It was not long before
such tragedies were to become commonplace, though often kept
secret at the time for the sake of 'the exigencies of war', which could
cover practically anything.

This impartial news-reading was already standard at the BBC
but it became significant when so much of the world depended on
London for the truth. The very fact that no emphasis was laid
anywhere, but that the utterances of Mr Chamberlain, Herr Hitler,
or Signor Mussolini were given equal weight, proved in the end to
be of inestimable value to the integrity of the BBC's word which
became universally believed.

The purveyors of this standard English and method of
announcing were during the war to become famous to the nation by
name and voice. Hitherto announcers were purely anonymous
figures, even their voices often sounding quite alike because of the
uniform manner of speaking. When the threat of war loomed
darkly it suddenly became necessary to name the announcers, so
that their voices would be instantly recognisable as those of friends
and tellers of the truth. These pre-war voices were those of Stewart
Hibberd, Alvar Liddell, Edward Ward (afterwards a noted war
correspondent), Joseph McLeod, Duncan Grinnell-Milne (who had
made a famous escape when a World War I prisoner of the
Germans), Frank Phillips, Lionel Marson and David Lloyd-James.
The latter were both old Haileyburians and by a curious co-
incidence in the quinquennial school photograph of our era (1929-
1934) David and I were standing next to each other. He was the son
of Professor Lloyd-James, the BBC's phonetics expert (or
Professor Higgins of the day, who was a little puzzled in trying to

place me, perhaps because of my four years in Papua and Australia).

Stewart Hibberd was the senior announcer and his rank seemed to travel with him as a discreet aura. He was softly spoken and his voice was thin and slightly husky (he was a very good tenor), and he had a graciously dignified manner. His approval was said to be signalled by the offer of an apple brought up from his West Country garden: 'Do have an apple, dear boy.' I was afforded this honour once. It seemed like an accolade and I felt ridiculously pleased.

There is a lovely story about Stewart, often told and I am not convinced that it is apocryphal. When King George V lay dying at Sandringham in January 1936, a colleague of Stewart's at the BBC went to the lavatory and settled himself in one of the cubicles pondering his thoughts. He suddenly became very aware of a well-known voice issuing from the cubicle next door: 'This *is* London' it intoned, then disapprovingly 'no, no – let me see – ah – This is *Lon*don – no . . . no . . . no . . . no' and finally 'This is London – ah – yes . . . yes . . . yes'. Stewart clearly was in mixed throes, searching for the appropriate inflections for the coming announcement to the nation.

The most impeccable of all BBC voices of this period, listened to almost with reverence by many, was that of Alvar Liddell. Half Swedish, he seemed to have something of the cold north in his delivery, which was immaculate. Every word could be clearly heard and nothing was unduly stressed. Another excellent wartime newsreader was Frank Phillips, his voice being easily identifiable by its slight fruitiness. He, too, had a very good singing voice. Though before the war, after serving for some years as an announcer in the BBC's early days at Savoy Hill, John Snagge had been employed in Outside Broadcasts, on its outbreak he became head of presentation and was one of the most important voices for delivering communiques of gravity. His voice was perfect for any pomp and circumstance and was very resonant, the effect being to give immense significance to his utterances. It was he who gave the first news of Operation Overlord and the D-Day landings.

All this time the dogs of war were clearly being unleashed and nearly everyone felt the concern of where duty should lie. Brought up as I had been on stories of the gallantry of my mother's brothers in the First World War, I began worrying about what to do next. I was on a six-month's probation with the BBC and did not want to fall foul of that. One possible solution to my quandary was suggested when one day Victor Cazalet asked me to go to Queens with him to watch the London Grass Court Championship semi-finals. During the day he told me that he was raising a Territorial Light Ac-Ac battery, to be based at Sevenoaks, and he suggested that I join them. Obviously that required some thinking about.

I had met Victor in Australia when he was out there with Lord Lothian at the Disarmament Conference and had wanted someone to give him a game of squash. He was then the British Amateur and Open Champion (equivalent in those days to Champion of the World) and I, having recently won the New South Wales title, was put up as a sacrificial lamb.

I remember only three other things about that day at Queens. The first occurred when driving in Victor's Rolls, and he suddenly said 'Oh, there's old Duff [Cooper]', and I saw a small insignificant but dapper figure, clad in the dress of the day, topped by a bowler. He looked somewhat sad as he waved 'hallo', perhaps because he had lately resigned from the Government in protest at the Munich sell-out. Then at Queens I saw Gottfried von Cramm, that brilliant stroke-player, beat Bobby Riggs 6/0, 6/1, with seemingly effortless ease. He then won the final comfortably but was not allowed (by Hitler so it was understood) to play at Wimbledon the following week since he had offended the Nazi regime. Later it was rumoured that Bobby Riggs, ever to show himself a canny fellow, knowing that von Cramm would not be able to play, had allowed him to win so easily at Queens in order to lengthen his own Wimbledon odds. He is said to have bet heavily upon himself, winning not only the Singles but the Men's Doubles and Mixed Doubles as well. It was the only year Riggs competed at Wimbledon and so became the only player with a perfect record in all three events.

The third incident was the most important to me at the time. Victor had spent some time in the dressing room talking to von Cramm, whom he knew well, and suddenly he turned to me and said 'I am sorry, Max I don't have time to give you a lift now. Do you mind making your own way?' Of course I could not as a very junior person (it mattered a lot in those days) say that I minded, although in fact I did – very much. This was because I was still undergoing my training as an announcer with the national and regional services, and, there were frequently long gaps in my duties. That was the case this day and I had only gone to Queens because there was a three- or four-hour interval between two jobs and Victor had promised to drive me back.

My next duty was to announce one of the very early 'ITMA'

shows at Maida Vale. Some of you will recognise these very popular initials as standing for *It's That Man Again*, featuring the great Tommy Handley. So, here was I, having to find my own way to the studios. I should have taken a taxi, of course, if I could have found one but, having been schooled never to take a taxi except *in extremis* (I had not yet realised that I was), I set off by underground. It was not long before I realised that I was not going to make it and you can imagine the panic that arose in the breast of a young BBC tyro still 'on probation'.

In desperation I resorted to what then (unbelievable now) was extreme behaviour. I actually turned to my neighbour in the tube and asked 'Excuse me, are you getting out soon?' He looked at me askance, wondering if I were depraved. The question probably decided him to say 'Yes' and I asked him, 'Would you please make a telephone call for me, here's the tuppence. Please ring the BBC, ask for the announcers' room and tell them that Max Robertson may not be at Maida Vale in time to announce 'ITMA'.' Giving me a very scared look he snatched the tuppence and the doors clanged behind him.

Apparently he did his Good Samaritan job and it was arranged that one of the announcers at Broadcasting House would announce the programme from there and the show was started by remote cue. A by-product of this high drama, or so it felt to me, was that interest in the announcers' room became so acute (as to whether I would make it in time or not) that Alvar Liddell forgot his own programme!

The BBC was in 1939 still a very sedate place. The aura of its great sculptor, Sir John Reith (although he had departed a year earlier) shrouded every aspect of the Corporation. The chief administrator, his title I now forget, was famous for the control he had over each individual. It was the classic arcane society with concentric ring upon ring jealously guarding the 'inner circle', with inward connections very limited indeed. I remember a lovely bit of verse written in *Aerial*, the BBC staff magazine, entitled 'Mr. Pym Passes By', relating to the huge influence that he wielded though he was rarely seen.

My efforts, so soon after I had been accepted as a fledgling announcer, to start doing running commentaries must have appalled the high priests as being the wildest temerity from one so junior and so young. Besides, one just didn't move out of one's chosen compartment – at least not for years. It wasn't done.

I had brought back some wax recordings, as they then were, of commentaaries I had done for the ABC on tennis and rugger, and I applied to do tennis commentary in the hope of getting some outside broadcasting. The head of the department, Seymour de Lotbiniere – a six-foot-seven mild-looking old Etonian – gave me an interview. He was known everywhere as Lobby by the staff and colleagues alike. His office, as I remember it, was then at the end of a balcony in an annexe of Broadcasting House, and outside it in 'open plan' sat famous people like John Snagge, Michael Standing, Wynford Vaughan-Thomas and Tommy Woodroffe (of recent ill-fated *The Fleet's Lit Up* fame). Going through their ranks as they sat looking you over with amusement or disdain was quelling enough but when you came into Lobby's den you quailed even more before his mild manner.

One soon came to recognise his favourite way of introducing any criticism – it was a shredding machine for any conceit. 'I don't quite understand. . .' Lobby would say and then take you quietly through your latest commentary (I am jumping ahead a few years) and tick off the points that he did not quite understand. You left with your tail between your legs, not quite understanding either why you even existed.

I remember once being in a delirium of delight when in 1948, having single-handed done a day's commentary on a Davis Cup match, against Sweden, under the greatest difficulties from a Stockholm rooftop at an oblique angle approximately 100 yards from the court, I returned to my hotel to find a cable which read, 'Well done – Lobby'. Joy was partially dissipated by the knowledge that, had it not been for Lobby's well-known quirk of parsimony on behalf of the BBC, the congratulations, brief though they were, would have been followed by 'but I did not quite understand. . .'.

Reverting to 1939, Lobby was a fairminded man, so granted me a commentary test at Wimbledon. I arrived, eager to show what I could do, and reported to Michael Standing. When live trans-mission ended, he took me up to the Centre Court box. He and Freddie Grisewood, who had been doing the commentary, sat in while I did my test – and this was unnerving in itself. I had not been told what match I would be given, so not only had I done no homework but I was totally unprepared for the names I had to deal with. It turned out to be a fourth round ladies' single between lefthanded Peggy Scriven (who had twice won the French title but was now past her best) and a Polish girl of solid certainty in her forehand wallop but complete insecurity for me in the pronunciation of her name, which was Jadwiga Jedrezejowska.

What I did not know was that in the tennis fraternity she was simply called Jed. Coming from Australian broadcasting, I did not use the prefix 'Miss', as in those days the BBC still did but, even with that slight advantage, I was quite unable to cope with her surname, repeatedly hiccuping on the second or third syllable – rather as in the last year or two I have with Slobadan Zivojinovic. Somehow I struggled through the test, giving I hope some impression that I knew a bit about the game and how to describe it, but in the words of a song of the day, 'It was a-a-a-a-gony'! For the record, Jed won 6/3, 6/2. What Lobby thought of the test I never discovered for soon war was to intervene.

When it became increasingly clear that war was imminent, knowing now that flying was not for me, I had decided to follow up that suggestion which Victor Cazalet had made to me at Queens. So it was that on 1 September 1939, after first reading the news of Hitler's shameful attack on defenceless Poland on the Empire Service early morning bulletin – I took the train to Sevenoaks and walked up the road to enlist in His Majesty's Service.

5

'GOING BUSH'

MY ARMY EXPERIENCE WAS UNDISTINGUISHED AND FRUSTRATING. AFTER SERVING IN THE RANKS ON GUNSITES DURING THE BATTLE of Britain, and a spell at Officer Cadet Training Unit, I was posted to the Maritime Anti Aircraft. (later to be the Maritime Royal Artillery), which supplied gunners for the defence of merchant ships. Unfortunately there was seldom a sea-going job for an officer. The only time I achieved this was as the technical adviser when a C.O.I. film was being made of these soldier sailors. Later I was Officer Commanding 5th Maritime Independent Troop R.A. for 'Operation Overlord', the invasion of Hitler's Europe. However, we were almost superfluous as Hitler, thoroughly convinced by the Allied deception plans that the main attack would be in the Pas de Calais, did not unleash the expected air strikes against the mass of shipping supplying the Normandy beach-heads.

Earlier, in my frustration at desk jobs, and wanting desperately to prove myself and pay something back, I had written a paper on 'Frontline Broadcasting', and had sent a copy to Lobby, who was then in charge of BBC war reporting. As a result he had applied for my secondment as a War Reporter but the War Office, in the shape of George Ewart, the major who administered the M.R.A. had – to my fury and dismay – turned the request down. If only I hadn't rushed into the army in the first place. Anyway, in answer to the question 'Daddy, what did you do in the war?', I can only answer, 'I was a soldier-sailor, who tinker-tailored'.

On my return to the BBC I found I had been confirmed as an established staff member. When I saw the appointments officer about getting back to work after my demob leave in February 1946, he asked me what I wanted to do and I immediately requested to go into Outside Broadcasts under Lobby. This was refused as the department was full, Lobby having just promised a job to a young Etonian wartime Guards officer, who had impressed war correspondents Wynford Vaughan-Thomas and Stewart MacPherson with his personality. His name was Brian Johnston. However, one of my old trainee announcing colleagues, Gibson Parker, had risen to be director of European Productions and asked for me to come back there as a producer of the famous magazine programme *London Calling Europe*. It was arranged also between him and Lobby that any outside broadcasts and commentaries that the European Service initiated in English I would be allowed to do. The European Service had been based for most of the war at Bush House, or 'Bush' as it was – most-affectionately – known. Here I was to spend a very happy and productive four years.

Like the all-round broadcasting experience I had been fortunate enough to get with the Australian Broadcasting Commission, the European Service was a marvellous training and practice ground. Whatever the event, I was there, covering things like football (regularly), ceremonials such as the Victory Parade, the Cenotaph Service on Remembrance Day, the Lord Mayor's Show, royal openings, departures and arrivals, the wedding of Princess Elizabeth, odd events like the 800th Anniversary of St Bartholomew's Hospital, the warm rivalry of Allied Forces' teams in the Britannia Shield Competition, cricket, the Varsity rugger match and so on. I was also one of the two regular producers of *London Calling Europe*, so that one met, auditioned and rehearsed a variety of speakers – most of them famous or specialist experts. I felt I was at the heart of events and generally I was having a very interesting and stimulating time.

My marriage to Nancy had come to an end – a casualty of wartime separations, the wrong difference in our ages and my selfish youth; so I threw myself wholeheartedly into my work, gaining wide and invaluable experience. Soon I was put in charge of all the other language commentators when we went to an event. In those days recordings were antedeluvian by today's standards. A mobile recording car would meet us at the venue. The discs were wax and could only be used once before being re-surfaced; the longest one could talk for on a single disc was about three and a half minutes. However, normally the cars were equipped with two turntables, so

that recording could be continuous. With my string of commentators I would descend on a football venue and we would draw
lots for the 'running order' during the match. Depending on how
many of us there were each man would have approximately one
disc's worth to let fly on in his own language; if there were only a
few of us we might get one in each half of the match. Sometimes it
was quite difficult to stop a commentator who was in full flight,
especially if an exciting movement was developing on the field and
he was oblivious that his recording time had run out. It was pure
luck as to whether anyone got a goal during their turn. It fell to me
to do the timing and shunting of the last man out to allow the next
man in. You had to be firm. You also had to be seen to be fair and
not take longer yourself – not always easy.

It was on one of these excursions – to the Lord Mayor's show –
that the ultimate in the ridiculous occurrred. Our commentator for
the Russian Service was a very likable and ebullient man called
André Mikhelsen. Because of the immediate postwar sensitivity of
the situation *vis-a-vis* Russia, Mikhelsen's non-sporting commentaries had to be written and passed beforehand. They were then
narrated at the actual event against the authentic sound background. We had an excellent position to view the procession, being
on a rooftop ledge just outside Mansion House. It was a cold,
windy day and when it came to Mikhelsen's stint he was happily
holding the script in one hand and the microphone in the other.
Facing over the procession as it passed around the square, he poured
forth what seemed to be a very reasonable and spontaneous
description, very often gesticulating to make his point. Suddenly
the wind became too blustery and he quite naturally shifted round
to hold his script against the wall, continuing to read it while facing
away from what was going on. This was noticed by various
sightseers on nearby vantage points. They started tittering with
laughter and the whole scene bcame a complete farce when an extra
fierce gust wrenched the next page from Mikhelsen's grasp and sent
it fluttering away while his face registered the most appalled dismay
I have ever seen. Some of the other onlookers nearly fell off their
perches.

On another occasion the European Service had put in its bid to
cover the speech of Bernard Shaw (the great GBS) to the serried
ranks of St Pancras Council on the occasion of his ninetieth
birthday. The Council were to present him with the freedom of the
borough where he had been a councillor himself in the early part of

the century. Home News had apparently not been interested in the event until the day before, when GBS fell off a chair and broke a leg, whereupon he imperiously summoned the BBC to his bedside to record his speech, so that the Council would not be disappointed on the morrow. Shaw was known as the 'shyest' possible person to persuade to broadcast. He would never give an interview. Suddenly Broadcasting House was alert and Home News loftily said they would be sending their representative, Brian Bliss, to do the job. However, European Service pride took a hand and our bosses said, 'Not on your life. We were first in on this event and our man Robertson is perfectly capable of recording Mr Shaw.' So it was left to yours apprehensively.

I arrived for the appointment and was received at Shaw's flat in Whitehall Court by his dragon, Miss Patch (she had been his secretary for thirty years). She escorted me to his small and quite spartan bedroom. She opened the door to reveal a truly awe-inspiring figure, as might have been described by Pliny, *'senex promissa barba, horrenti capillo'* (an old man with a long beard and rough hair), sitting bolt upright in bed and fixing me with the most penetrating gaze I had experienced since being told my fortune.

This was a rush job and the recording car that had been booked for it had only a single turntable, which meant that only three and a half minutes at a time could be recorded. I explained this to GBS who nodded testily and the sound engineer pushed the mike and its cable through the window and eventually let us know he was ready. His name was 'Skipper' Arnell, known as Skip, and he was one of the three or four battle-hardened engineers who had accompanied the war reporters. He was also a Cockney with a large chip on his shoulder, never losing an opportunity to make his presence felt. When we got the go-ahead I gave Shaw a hand cue and he started. I have never been so impressed in my life by any performance. Clearly the old man had thought about it, but he ad libbed in his marvellous English with the well-known Irish accent, giving his message with clarity and noble wording. He had only been going for a minute when Skip gave the usual remote signal to draw the attention of the performers when something had gone wrong. He made the equivalent of an electronic raspberry on the line, following it up in his Cockney tones with 'I'm sorry Mr Shaw, you'll have to start again, I've had swarf trouble.' (Swarf was the wax ribbon produced as the needle cut a disc – too much could cause a surface hissing.) The ninety-year-old took it without a quiver.

Nor was there a quaver in his voice when he started reproducing what he had said, almost word for word and, with two more stops for change of record, completed the notable eleven minute recording without faltering and with perfect syntax. It was perhaps the greatest bit of broadcasting I have ever witnessed.

Before the event, while we were waiting for Skip to set up everything I had plucked up the courage to ask what I knew I must – would the great man give me an interview afterwards? He had immediately said no rather crossly, and with a slight sense of relief I had not pursued the matter. With the recording done he clearly relaxed a bit and, perhaps thinking that here was a young man who ought to be given a chance, showed that he was a generous-hearted person. 'That interview you asked me for,' he said, 'I might consider it, if you will send me the questions in writing, but they must be answerable on a postcard.'

I went back to Bush House agog with anticipation. Here was the chance to get an interview that nobody had ever had. It seemed to me much too big an affair to handle by myself, so I told my boss who told his boss and so it went on up the ladder until word came back from on high: 'Ask Mr Shaw the following questions.' I wrote to GBS with the questions which seemed to me to be rather portentous and received a forthright postcard to the effect that each of these questions would require at least 20,000 words to answer. 'Unless we can contrive some cut-and-thrust the proposal is off.' Note the words 'we' and 'cut-and-thrust'. I was both flattered and appalled. However, it was now up to me, so with the help of some friends I sat down and worked out a list of some ten questions, all of which were short and all of which I felt gave Shaw the chance to make one of his famous pithy aphorisms or epigrams in reply. Back came another postcard in the great man's handwriting. 'These questions cannot be answered in under 200 words.' At least I had done better than the big white chiefs!

On rejoining the BBC, for the first time since leaving school I started to play cricket regularly, mostly with the BBC First XI; but I also had one or two games with the West Indies Wanderers from whom Leary Constantine (later to be Jamaica's first High Commissioner to Britain after Independence), Ken Ablack and Bertie Clarke amongst others played. I was the wicketkeeper and my first experience of keeping to Bertie, who in 1939 had been a Test match spinner, was exhilarating. The wicket was a little soft and so taking bite and turn. Bertie had a tremendous top-spin and those batsman who played forward either gave him a caught and bowled or missed the ball and lifted their back foot. I had three stumpings and felt marvellous.

Leary Constantine, though past his prime, was still quite fast – and very difficult to bat or keep wicket to. His action was unique, for he waved his bowling hand around in the air as he ran up to the wicket, with the result that neither batsman nor wicketkeeper could sight the ball properly, leaving both with a most disconcerting feeling of uncertainty.

Bertie, who did freelance radio work for programmes to the West Indies, also turned out regularly for the BBC and I suppose over the years I kept wicket to him more than any other keeper, since I played for the BBC First XI for twenty years. He was a marvellous bowler. Once he took all ten wickets, including the last three as a hat-trick. He did not turn the ball a lot but he had this prodigious top-spin that made it lift. Although I kept to him so regularly, I was never able to 'read' his googly with any certainty, for he had at least three different finger-spin actions for it. He had so much spin that he made the ball zzzzz like an angry bee in the air, a terrifying sound to any batsman and one which I have never heard any other bowler produce. The only ball that I could always tell for certain – and it was just as well that I could – was his quickie. It was venomous – a yorker swinging from off to leg stump and quite devastating to the normal club batsman. In those days it very rarely missed the wicket but I prided myself, standing up as I was, that I never let any byes off it. The secret was that one suddenly saw much more of the back of his right hand as he took a firm grasp on the ball when running up. Then it flashed over like a cobra striking.

Some three to four months after I had re-started with the BBC I came in one morning to look at the production sheet showing the contributors for that day's *London Calling Europe* and saw the name of J Hampden Jackson on the list. Surely it was not possible that this was my old mentor and tormentor as history master at Haileybury? The master whose last report on me had read 'I pity his tutor at Cambridge'; the man who had done more to influence Haileyburians of the day (in my last year, 1934, these included Christopher and Patrick Mayhew) to the left in the wave of socialist idealism that was engulfing the youth of the day, prompted by the extremes of suffering of the unemployed as exemplified in the 'Hunger Marches'. Jackson, in his brilliant efforts to stimulate progressive thought, often came out with exaggerated pronouncements, many of which I felt were outrageous and tearing down much of the tradition I revered. So I always sat stony-faced at his sallies when everyone else was roaring with laughter. He must have considered me a horrible little prig.

So when reception telephoned up to my office to announce his arrival I did something I have never done before or since to anyone – I deliberately kept him waiting for five minutes before sauntering down to the reception hall. I then greeted him in my best BBC official manner with 'Mr Hampden Jackson, I believe. Do come this way to the studio.' Alas for my rather pompous revenge, we had only walked a few yards down the corridor when he asked 'Were you by any chance at Haileybury?' and I was immediately disarmed and defenceless. We got on very well and he actually confided to me that he was now a Tory.

It was a very cosy existence at Bush House. Everyone still seemed imbued with the wartime spirit. We worked long hours for the fun and interest of it without any thought of asking for days off in lieu. Most of the staff were veterans of the wartime service. It was a wonderful polyglot hotchpotch of people. There was plenty of temperament but also much laughter and good temper, and there were not many who refused to co-operate or go out of their way to do a good turn.

It was the best possible anodyne for me at a difficult time, keeping me from thinking too much on a personal level and giving me wonderful breadth and depth in broadcasting experience. I remember covering the 'Britain Can Make It' exhibition in September that year and doing at least forty interviews in one day. Somebody, knowing that I was going to have a tough day, had given me a couple of purple hearts, those amphetamines which were a derivative of the pills given to airmen to keep them awake on long bombing raids. With my natural Scot's caution I had taken half of one. It certainly gave me energy and, I felt, clarity of mind but, having used it again once or twice I soon came to the conclusion that it was dangerous and could lead the mind into uncontrolled thought. I quickly gave them up.

So the busy and very mixed life ran on, finding me jumping from sport to industrial visits, to ceremonials – back to a different sport and so on. Certainly there was a strong sensation of being part of living history and one got so used to being in privileged seats, rather than having to queue (as well as pay!), that nowadays I very seldom find I want to go to an event privately. I suppose I was getting thoroughly spoiled.

During 1947 I was making many new friends and widening the scope of my broadcasting experience. One figure coming easily to mind is that of Clifford Troke – a most endearing gnome of a man with a solid body, large nose, and a determination to get to the bottom of anything. He was our science correspondent and started the programme called *Science Review*, for which I often found myself contributing pieces in the form of a commentary or interview, on some technical process. It worked quite well, for if I could be made to understand it I could repeat it for the listener in a layman's terms. I sometimes narrated the programme, as I also did *London Calling Europe* if my other half, Tony Brown, was producing. I was quite in demand for narration, having a clear voice, and usually did the linking for any big programme such as the end of the year review.

Following a wide variety of sports as I did, I soon came to the notice of Angus Mackay, who was in charge of all news sports programmes for 'Home' and 'Light' as the two domestic networks were then called. I'll never forget the first time Angus asked me to do a piece for him. It was a report on some minor tennis tournament and he told me he wanted three minutes. I put my heart and soul into this and wrote a careful script. On my arrival at the studio in Broadcasting House in time for rehearsal, Angus said to me 'I'm sorry, Max, I've had to cut you to two and a half'. I spent the next quarter of an hour editing out what I hoped were the least of my pearls. I was on the air reading the result when a hand slid a note in front of me, saying, 'Do three and a half'. Afterwards I decided that never again would I write a script for Angus. Nor did I. Indeed, I became quite adept at ad libbing to an exact time, which made it easier to contract or expand to order – a necessary skill when working for Angus.

He was noted as a very strong character and one who was extremely loyal to his faithful servants. After *Saturday Evening Sports Parade* he always took his flock off to the George and held court there. I was not a drinker and found this very difficult, toying with a shandy and listening to the conversation of the great sports columnists, such as Jim Manning, Jim Wicks and Peter Wilson. This relationship with Angus continued happily for a long time; he found me a useful odd job man since I was here, there and everywhere and there was no fee involved because I was on the staff.

It all ended sadly when, after I had been a freelance for some while, my overall contract with the BBC was renewed and laid down certain fees that I should get for different types of broadcasting. My fee for a report on tennis was increased from three to five guineas. Angus steadfastly continued to pay me three guineas. For a while I suffered this, knowing that he was a difficult man if you crossed him and enjoying the work as I did. Eventually, feeling perhaps that it was rather unfair, and that I should have my 'rights' since it was the BBC who had granted this fee, I requested it from Angus. He made it quite clear that he had no intention of paying it. So I had to stand on my dignity and he did not use me again. Not long afterwards I ruefully became aware that he had increased his standard fee for all contributors to five guineas! Perhaps I should have been more patient. Or perhaps I was the guinea pig, from whose misfortune everybody else benefited.

Being the BBC representative at an event – even if only for the European Service – gave me the immediate 'in' and I suppose it was very easy to begin to feel that this was right and proper. I am sure there must have been occasions when I could have appeared to be arrogant as a result of this but I hope I did not sin too often.

In early October 1947 I was given what turned out to be – for me – a momentous assignment. When I arrived at the Conservative Party Conference at the Brighton Dome, however, I had no idea that there would be more significance in it than my first glimpse – in the flesh – of the great Winston Churchill, leader of the party. He was also to receive the freedom of the borough. I was in my usual guise of team-leader – *Gauleiter* some often thought – for the European 'circus'. I had no pretensions to political knowledge. So this was a new world for me, and for the Conservative party, which was trying to rebuild its bridges with the voters after the cataclysmic disaster of the postwar election of 1945, it was a very serious one. I had to do a report in English as well as see that the language commentators got their material. Somehow I managed to concoct something that seemed passable and when I put it down the line to Bush House there was no adverse comment.

It had been a long day and I was rather tired when I had to attend a cocktail party for the press. It was really something of a cocktail-*dansant*. I had always been terrified of dancing, never having succeeded in learning more than a few faltering steps and I always avoided it where at all possible. Apparently I was skulking on the edge of the floor, looking rather abject, as I often do when I am perfectly content but concentrating on something else. My contemplation was interrupted by a charming, bubbling and very pretty girl with a sweet smile, that really did curl up the corners of her mouth in a cupid's bow, who came up and asked me to dance. I was completely taken aback and went quietly!

She was one of the secretaries working at the Conservative Party Central Office and had been detailed to help with the PR. She told me afterwards that her 'Gauleiter' had said to her, 'Liza, for heaven's sake go and look after that miserable-looking chap from the BBC'. Her name was Elisabeth Beresford, who later was to achieve fame as creator of The Wombles, and although I didn't realise it at the time, this was my first meeting with the girl who was to be my second wife.

6

DOWN THE CRESTA

As the year 1947 drew on we became increasingly mindful that next year was to see the first Olympic Games since 1936. The winter Olympics would come first and they were to be in St Moritz. Early in the year instinct had told me that I would do well to take a skiing holiday, which I did in the well-known Swiss resort of Murren. I was not a born skier, being stiff, having poor balance and plenty of natural caution. By the end of the fortnight I still could not perform a christie turn, which was the only sure way of stopping – except by deliberately falling as I frequently had to do. But I made contacts with some of the winter sports leaders – especially Sir Arnold Lunn who was the doyen of downhill skiing. It occurred to me that it might be a good idea to break new ground and try to become the BBC's first winter sports commentator, so on my return I wrote a report which was passed on to Lobby. I tried to outline how best I felt a ski race could be covered.

Luckily for me this groundwork and my report paid off. I was rewarded by being told that not only would I be representing the European Service in English (my normal right now), but also that the Home and Light programmes, radio Newsreel and any of the news services would take specialist bits offered to them and would use parts of my European contributions as suited them. So, when the time came I would be covering for the whole of BBC radio, whilst also being used piecemeal by television.

But before this I was given the job of training the various language commentators in the techniques of trying to cover skiing events. To this purpose we would watch a lot of old film of the 1936

Olympics shot by the great Leni Riefenstahl and the various commentators, many of whom were newscasters detailed to do this as a sideline, would try their paces and get some experience of the problems involved and how to overcome them. Some of them, much to their own surprise, turned out to be pretty good. This training was later carried on in the spring and summer of 1948 for the Summer Olympics, when it was much easier to conjure up real life situations for the aspiring commentators. One of the films I remember we used constantly was the 1500 metres at Los Angeles in 1932. It was won by that great New Zealand runner, Dr Jack Lovelock, whom I met and interviewed at this time. The man who came second in Los Angeles was Jack Cornes, the British champion and eldest brother of an old friend of mine, Stella Cornes. I so clearly remember wanting him to win at the time and the disappointment when he just failed. Now, watching the race time and time again I always suffered the frustration of seeing him beaten. Every time I found myself willing him to win, as if a miracle might happen.

So when the time came I was literally 'Our Man in St Moritz'. What a marvellous mandate it was to have! I don't think I have ever worked so hard or pleasurably in my life. I was here, there and everywhere with a faithful Swiss engineer, Monsieur Mérinat, attached to me. He was rubicund, open-faced and cheerful. He did not mind what he did nor how long it took and, as we whizzed from event to event, he began to be more and more infected by the madness I carried with me. Everything was new and shining bright, the weather perfect, the snow and ice glittering. The gladiators in these sports were fascinating and so contrasting – from the grace of the ice-skating (the American Dick Button's leaps were electrifying and Canadian Barbara Anne Scott was like a fairy on the top of an iced cake) to the skill and daring of the downhill skiers and jumpers – the nerveless Cresta riders and bobsleighers, the sheer guts and stamina of the long distance skiers, the rugged power and dash allied to the skill of the ice-hockey players.

Postwar television was still very young and representing them was the first head of Outside Broadcasts, Ian Orr-Ewing (now Lord Orr-Ewing) who had a camera team with him. However, I was also much in demand from him for interviews and bits of commentary on the Cresta and bobsleigh. The European 'circus' was under the command of Konrad Syrop, a lovely man, a native Pole who had all their best qualities. There were countless language representatives covering for their various countries. Charles Roetter, one of the top scriptwriters in the English service (his scripts would be translated into the other languages for broadcast from Bush House), was also there. My wide-eyed naive innocence and sheer joy at being present on such a marvellous occasion – away from the dreary rationing and petty restrictions of post-war Britain – was given a sudden jolt when Charles and Konrad took me aside and said 'Max, what is your "angle" on all this?' I literally had no idea what Charles meant, not having been brought up as a journalist. He tried to explain to me, but I found it very difficult. I still do. Why should anything have a slant to it, instead of just being itself as you see and feel it?

Before coming out to St Moritz I had done my best to get to know the leading personalities and officials in each of the sports and had covered some of the preparatory events. The sport that was most immediately compelling to anyone with any sense of adventure was the Cresta. This is individual to St Moritz and was not strictly part of the Olympic Games but what is known as a 'demonstration sport'. Every venue of an Olympic Games, Summer or Winter, is allowed to present its own native demonstration sport. It is a nice idea for it spreads the gospel and sport, whatever it be, is better than war.

The Cresta is a toboggan run built afresh every year by specialists, who in this case were Italian craftsmen, out of ice blocks. It is contoured down the valley and each year, since it is handcrafted, it is slightly different. It has vintage years like wines and even the most experienced riders would have to get to know the new quirks of the current course. I said 'toboggan' run; that is a terrible understatement because there is nothing else anywhere in the world like the Cresta. For one thing you do not go down sitting on your posterior; you go lying flat on your face and when the speed gets up to sixty mph plus with your nose only inches from the ground you feel as if you are travelling through the sound barrier.

Whenever I could I used to return to watch the Cresta, even if I was not reporting on it, and I soon got to know the leading riders and in particular, Colonel Jimmie Coats who was the non-riding captain of the British team, though in the past he had been one of the best. The president of the club was the formidable Lord Brabazon who had been Minister for Aircraft Production during vital war years and an excellent rider himself. Ian Orr-Ewing was his nephew, so he, too, naturally gravitated towards the Cresta. After a while, having had so much to do with it, it began to be borne in on me that I had to go down myself or forever lose face. Until the Games actually ended I had every excuse not to. Firstly because I was too busy and secondly because I could not afford to get hurt. However, when the last Sunday arrived I knew I had to go down.

Beginners did not ride the full course, nor attempt a running start ending by throwing themselves face down onto the 'skeleton', as the toboggan was called, but set off from about two- fifths of the way down at a point called 'Junction'. Booted, helmeted and spurred (thought the latter were on the toe-caps, not the heels), wishing that I had been morally brave enough not to go, completely apprehensive of the whole experience and my mind nearly numb with fear, I did not take in a last minute piece of advice from Jimmie Coats: 'Now, don't forget, rake all the way,' (meaning with my toe-caps down in the ice). 'It doesn't matter how long it takes.' And then ominously, 'We want you to get down in one piece'. The record from Junction was then 45.2 seconds – I was not out to beat it. Lying spreadeagled on the skeleton, with the seat back, I felt like a landed fish for I already seemed to have gone through a nightmare struggle to get myself there. All beginners went with the sliding seat back, for then the weight was at the rear of the skeleton and the teeth at the back of the runners also bit into the ice to help braking.

I was pushed off and was beginning to gather some speed when suddenly into my frozen comprehension there penetrated an anguished shout from Jimmie, 'R . . . a . . . a . . . ke!' he yelled. I have always had pretty quick reactions (you don't play a game of rackets or attempt a Wimbledon commentary without them) but never have they been as instantaneous as they were then. My toe-caps shot down into the ice with such force that I almost stopped dead. From then on they remained firmly embedded but nevertheless the speed began to grow. By the time I had rounded the famous Battledore and Shuttlecock (the scene of many a disaster for both experts and novices alike) and was entering the straight, the nerve-racking experience was becoming so terrifying, the noise of the uncontrolled skeleton rattling down and the banging of it against the ice walls so overwhelming, that I seemed to be moving in a strange earthquake-like vortex that got faster and faster until it became a mighty wind. I felt that I was almost coming off several times but somehow, though bruised and battered from the bangs, I suddenly found myself through the bottom and coming up the finishing bank that braked the onward rush, until finally I was still – absolutely spent, literally gasping like the landed fish I had felt at the top. Then the loudspeaker clicked on and I heard my time – 94 seconds – over double the record but at least I was comforted by the knowledge that Errol Flynn had taken 120 on his first trip!

As soon as the ordeal was over there was a tremendous sense of exhilaration and achievement until, trudging up the road back to Junction, I realised that I *had* to do it again. On my second trip I was rather more aware of what was happening and also managed to hit the 'counters', as the sides were called, less often. As a result I was rewarded with 72.6, and the third time down things went better still – 62.4. Surely I had done enough for the flag to be kept flying? But, as I came up the hill, I met Ian who had also been going down. 'I'm not really trying on this one,' he said and went down in 60 dead. Some effort at not trying I thought bitterly to myself, or perhaps relaxation had brought him the result. I knew I had to do it once more.

This time Jimmie Coats said to me, 'Max, if you don't steer' – I had merely been giving the skeleton its 'head' – 'you are going to go over Shuttlecock.' The idea of this frightened me enough. I was determined I was going to beat Ian's time or die in the attempt. As I rounded Battledore and came towards Shuttlecock I knew I was going faster than before and remembered Jimmie's words. I managed to wrench the nose of the skeleton awkwardly around and just avoided going over the lip. As soon as I was past the dreaded point and into the staight, for the first time I slipped the seat forward so that there was no brake on the rear runners. The feeling of speed was amazing and suddenly in an almost divine exaltation I lost all fear – the acceleration was so great. The sensation of utter speed was the most wonderful I have ever experienced and when I finally came to a stop I waited with agonised anticipation. On came the loudspeaker stating in its nasal tone – '*fifty-nine point nine!*'

My euphoria was complete and I felt I could now hang up my skeleton; to do any more would be asking for trouble and I was genuinely too busy. I was rather glad that Isobel Roe, the captain of the ladies ski team, happened to witness all this, for I felt it might give me a little standing – which I certainly did not have as a result of my skiing.

Emboldened, I was determined to try to do a commentary going down the bob run. M. Mérinat was an enthusiastic collaborator but alas there was no equipment, for these were very early days in mobile recording. Luckily the captain of the British team was Group Captain Collings and he came to our rescue by arranging that we could borrow an RAF walkie-talkie set. It only had a short range but enough if M. Mérinat was stationed halfway down the course. So it was arranged and on a practice day after the championships were over we had a go.

The bob races are either for boblet, which is a two-man toboggan, or for bobsleigh – which is four-man. Obviously I could not go down on a boblet, for both men have vital jobs, one steering, the other braking – the brakeman being just as important, for his little touches on the brakes help the driver to keep the right line. The line is vital, for these events are sometimes won literally by hundredths of a second and the perfect line gives a far better chance of the fastest time. So, I was given the third seat just in front of the brakeman in a four-man bobsleigh. On this the two middle men have no real job, apart from adding weight and swaying tucked in with the other two to keep down wind resistance. Their main job is in being fast musclemen for the take-off, at which the bobsleigh is pushed as hard and as fast as possible, the crew jumping in at the last second as it is starting to gather real way.

The walkie-talkie was strapped to my chest with the batteries on my back, so I was able to cling on. Knowing that I would only have one chance, and wanting to do everything in my power to make the best of it, I had spent quite a while trying to memorise absolutely the map of the course, with the names of its sucessive bends, some of them like Snake, Sunny and Horseshoe being famous. Not only had I spent time memorising but I had 'walked' the course with the driver of the number one sleigh, trying to visualise each corner and landmark as it would come up. It was not as frightening an experience as going down the Cresta for the first time, because in the latter I had been responsible for myself, knowing that I was completely inexperienced. On the bobsleigh I was in the hands of experienced riders. So all that I had to do was to concentrate on my commentary and on keeping going.

There was much ribaldry and barracking beforehand and at the start, for I am quite sure many felt I would not be able to keep talking. This, as far as I know, was the first time anyone had tried to do such a thing. So, as you can imagine, I was determined to keep the flag – both my own and that of the BBC – flying.

We set off with the proper three crew members pushing me as well as the bob. I began blithely enough I felt, something like this:

'And now we begin the course with the RAF bob crew who took part in the Olympics, minus their number three, who has kindly allowed me to take his place. The weight of the bob is . . . the team are. . .' and I named them as they swung aboard. The bob was beginning to gather a little speed but as yet nothing.

As yet! My carefully memorised and prepared plan was soon being torn to shreds in my mind, for as the bob accelerated Sunny suddenly was rushing towards us with an exaggerated momentum. Breathing began to get difficult – I found myself clinging on for dear life to the handles, but uppermost in my mind was the knowledge that, if I stopped, I would never start again and I *must keep going*. At first what I said was reasonably coherent but as the speed grew and grew and the huge walls on the bends rushed at us like a vast ice surf about to break – and I felt the great G-forces as we went round them – my speech became a stuttering screaming gabble, in which a few words could be made out by any disinterested listener.

I was very aware of what I had been trying to say and afterwards could just about distinguish it. From a programme point of view the only thing that could be said for my performance was that it was a first and *I did keep going*! Since we were sitting, and not face down as on the skeleton, the sense of speed was perhaps not quite as great, nor the sensation of rushing into a black hole in space quite as desperate, but it was a tremendous experience and again there was that wonderful feeling of relieved exhilaration as the bobsleigh braked and came to a halt at the bottom of the run. Did I say that the sensation of speed was not as great as on the Cresta? Of course it was, because in my first ride on the Cresta I was averaging about half speed, braking all the way. On the bob, with an expert crew, there were no holds barred and our time was only a few seconds off the record. In a different way it had been quite as dramatic.

The result when we heard it was disappointing. Not only was my commentary hard to follow but it was not helped by the poor quality of the recording. This was partly caused by M. Mérinat's recording car being based amongst trees halfway down the course, and these were muffling the signal. However, I had done it and I believe it still exists in the BBC archives as the first time ever. I was to repeat it to better effect for TV at the next Winter Olympics in Oslo.

So I came home bruised to London a little bit like a conquering hero, having had the time of my life and feeling I had done the best job I could have for the BBC. This was reflected in many congratulations and memos from various departments, both domestic and European, thanking me for my efforts and telling me that they had been widely used. It had all been very much worthwhile.

7

New Frontiers

APART FROM COVERING A VARIETY OF SPORTS EVENTS — SUCH AS THE WINTER OLYMPICS FOR RADIO — I WAS ALSO, IN MY COMPARATIVELY few recreational hours, myself playing as much cricket for the BBC as possible. It was always very enjoyable, for it was taken seriously. I never particularly liked playing games when there was no real desire to win and the thing was being done for some lark or exhibition. Our captain at that time, Leo Bennett, was a fine batsman (he played for Northants for a season or two) and, coming in at first wicket down, he would immediately take charge. Colin Barker, who usually opened the innings with me, and I – whichever of us was not first out – always got a strange feeling of reluctance when Leo came in because we knew that from now on it was his show and it was just too easy for him to take a single off the last ball of the over and face the new one. Our role became largely passive as spectators.

That said, Leo was truly a very great club batsman and feared by our opponents. I remember one day we were having our annual 'blood' match with Malden Wanderers. I say 'blood' match because the two sides had come to dislike each other. Why was never quite clear, unless it was that we regarded them as too professional and too desirous of winning, or at least not losing. The Wanderers batted first and went on and on and on, piling up a very good score which, with any other side in a whole day game, would have meant a declaration sometime before tea. Not so with Malden Wanderers for they feared Leo's batting ability.

When we came in for tea and they at last declared, Leo looked like thunder. His answer was to send in not Colin with me but Len Phillips. Len, or Phil as we usually called him, was a fantastic batsman. He was also a very good wicketkeeper but did not mind in the least me keeping wicket, as he enjoyed fielding. As a bat he normally came in at about number six. Doing an Ian Botham type slog, he would make a quick forty to sixty runs and was therefore very useful. His method of batting, since he had a 'fair round belly' of some considerable girth, was always exactly the same – whatever the ball – except in one respect. He would advance his left foot and merely adjust the angle of his bat to the line of the ball. The stroke was then made by a convulsive heave of his tummy and more often than not it went for six. On this occasion after ten minutes the score read 54 for 1, last man 50. That was Phil – with some hurricane hitting. I had contributed four! Needless to say this had put us on time with the clock and we managed to win. As a result Leo dropped the fixture next year.

Another example of Phil's batting prowess occurred when in 1947 the BBC went on a cricket tour up in the Lake District. One of our players was Anthony Craxton, a studious, if not always successful bat with a long reach. He was also a guileful leg-spinner, who suffered from being in the shadow of Bertie Clarke. Later Anthony was to achieve BBC renown as the producer on TV not only of a lot of Test match cricket programmes – but also for coverage of royal occasions. He and his delightful wife, Anne, became great friends of mine. On this tour they invited me to come and stay with them at her father's house at Ellergreen, near Kendal. It was at Kendal, I think, that Phil's prowess came to its greatest fruition. It was a small and very attractive ground and Phil was merrily whacking his strokes and hitting glorious fours and sixes. The team we were playing against were in the local league, so that each time Phil reached fifty the cap came round. His score soared on, his century soon coming up, followed by 150 and each time the cap went round. When it came round again at 164 we could not understand why. He had broken the ground record, achieving a final score of 167 with some of the finest hitting I have ever seen.

However, the big sporting event to look forward to in everyone's calendar at that time was, of course, the first postwar Summer Olympics in 1948. As a result of the complicated preparations for these and all the work involved for Rex Alston (who in OB Department was in charge of most sports broadcasting), I was asked by Lobby to take over the arrangements for that year's

Wimbledon and was temporarily seconded by the European Service to do so. I had, of course, been at Wimbledon throughout the 1946/47 championships and, apart from commentating and reporting every day for the European Service, had frequently done commentaries for the domestic services. This time I was not only administratively in charge but was also doing commentary for the Home and Light programmes every day. This was the year that John Bromwich of Australia, that unusual player whose best years would have been during the war, reached the final against Bob Falkenburg of America (brother of the famous actress Jinx Falkenburg).

Falkenburg, too, was a most extraordinary player, being six foot three inches tall, very thin and loose and often giving the general effect of a drooping flower that has not the strength to hold its head up. He had a tremendous service (which many who had seen Vines play likened to his service), a big forehand and little else. He also seemed to lack stamina and was forever taking a rest between points, which in those days was considered unsporting. He even 'threw' games and sets to have a breather.

Bromwich was one of the three great unorthodox players that Australia had thrown up just before and after the war. They were: Vivian McGrath, the first to have a two-handed backhand at international level; John Bromwich a lefthander who served righthanded, and had a two-handed backhand; and Geoff Brown who, like Bromwich was a lefthander with a righthanded service (it was like the whirlwind of a small catherine wheel) and a two-handed backhand which was a great attacking weapon. Bromwich was also a brilliant doubles player, he and Adrian Quist eventually winning the Australian title eight times. He brought all his doubles guile to his singles play and to that end always had his rackets very loosely strung. He was the master of the oblique, especially the wrong-footer and his dropshots literally dropped like the pro-verbial poached egg – dead.

Bromwich was terribly nervous. After a fluctuating match, in which Falkenburg repeatedly stalled and took time off (sometimes sinking to his knees on the court in a flopped over position which on the air I christened the 'praying mantis') and had even thrown the second set to love, the score reached two sets all and 5/3 Bromwich serving. He got to match-point at 40/15. At this juncture the 'praying mantis' was doing his act repeatedly and clearly the delays were taking a toll on Bromwich's nerves. Falkenburg saved the first

67

match-point and Bromwich then missed a volley on the second. At advantage Bromwich had match point again, Falkenburg saving it with a good passing shot. After this Bromwich seemed to know, and certainly the crowd did, that he had missed his chance. He scarcely won another point. I don't think I have ever felt so sorry for a player, for if anyone ever deserved to win Wimbledon, John Bromwich did – and at the time many felt that Falkenburg did not.

No sooner was Wimbledon, a high experience for me, over, than I found myself flung into the Summer Olympic Games which this year took place in London. It was a tremendous honour – the first postwar Summer Olympics – and the excitement was immense. The last time the Olympics had been staged in London had been in 1908. For these Games I was working for the domestic services, with Rex Alston and Harold Abrahams, on the athletics.

I had been doing athletics for the European Service for the previous two years and so had seen quite a bit of Rex and Harold. Rex had been a considerable athlete and player of ball games himself, having played minor county cricket for Bedford and been a good rugger player; he'd also been second string to Harold Abrahams in the 100 and 220 yards at Cambridge. Harold was the last Briton to win the Olympic 100 metre title (in Paris in 1924) before Alan Wells repeated the feat in the Moscow Olympics in 1980. Harold was also the character whose life story was used (with that of Eric Liddell, the 400 metre winner in Paris that year in a world record time of 47.6 seconds) for that fabulous film *Chariots of Fire*.

Harold was an amazing man; trained in the law, he was very clever, with a brilliant sharp mind. His enthusiasm was unbounded but he was very sensitive – especially of any criticism (as most artists are) – and very generous, both with advice and help for a beginner in the field, as I was. His wife, Sybil, was a darling and the two were devoted to each other. As a result of his track achievements Harold was the BBC's original commentator for athletics but this role was now taken over principally by Rex and – for some of the quicker events – by me, while Harold did his masterly inside-knowledge summaries.

It was in that first postwar Olympics that the great Czechoslovakian athlete, Emil Zatopek, captured the imagination of the world with his extraordinary performances. He was the first man, probably, to demonstrate that the reserves of stamina created by pushing back the frontiers of endurance with punishing training such as no one had ever undertaken before, could transform an ordinary runner into a world beater. He did not look at all like an athlete in his running style, which was a sort of rolling, shambling gait with his head carried, as it seemed, almost on his left shoulder, his tongue lolling in and out and his left fist pumping up and down. In the 5000 metres he allowed the Belgian, Gaston Reiff, to get much too far ahead and left his own effort far too late. Even so, he very nearly caught him and would have done in another ten metres. When the Belgian glanced over his shoulder in the home straight, his unforgettable look of sudden triumphant realisation told all. He knew he could just hold on and get to the line first. Zatopek, however, made no such mistake in the 10,000 when he destroyed the field. He was one of the outstanding competitors of those Games. The other memorable figure was the blonde Dutch heroine, of great physical stature as so many of their women are, sprinter Fanny Blankers-Koen. She won four Gold medals and was the equivalent in a sense of Jesse Owens, the superb American sprinter and long jumper of the 1936 Games in Berlin. I interviewed Fanny and found her a charming and modest person, though I had to look up to her in every way.

When I was not actively engaged in radio with the athletics broadcasting team, I was borrowed once or twice by Ian Orr-Ewing for television. My first TV commentary ever was on the final of the 800 metres, won by Mal Whitfield of the United States, a very fine forceful runner with a majestic stride. But the most dramatic moment of the athletics was when the great Arthur Wint of Jamaica, whose team were the clear favourites for the 4 x 400 metres relay, suddenly fell to the track writhing and beating the ground with the baton, clearly suffering the most terrible cramp. It was a very painful and frightful moment for him physically and psychologically, feeling deeply as he did that he had let his team-mates down. Jamaica had some recompense when they won the event at Helsinki in 1952.

After the athletics were over, I was detailed to cover weight-lifting. Forewarned, I had been to the British trials and had tried to steep myself in as much of the lore of this strange sport as possible. It is not an easy sport to commentate on live on the air. I had to try to give the layman (which I was, too) a simple explanation of what is happening, while building up the atmosphere to the moment of 'attack'. I remember one competitor who brought himself to the boil, so to speak, by striding up and down in front of the bar and urging himself on with ferocious grunts. These quickened and deepened in tempo and sound until, at the moment of cresendo, he stooped, straddled, bent down and, seizing the bar, brought it up in one swift movement to the shoulders to complete the 'clean'. He steadied himself for a second and then – with a trumpet like a wild elephant – hoisted it up at arm's length above his head to complete the 'jerk'. Although it's not a sport I would have wished to continue covering, I did enjoy the experience at the time.

Those 1948 Summer Olympics were a remarkable effort by all concerned. A battered world was demonstrating a renewal of courage and optimism, and it was a privilege to be there – especially as London had been given the honour of staging the Games in recognition of Britain's war-time sacrifices for the free world.

8

THESE I HAVE KNOWN

I'D LIKE TO GIVE A LITTLE TIME NOW TO ONE OR TWO OF THE PERSONALITIES I MET AND THE PROFESSIONALS I WORKED WITH. I'VE mentioned Skip Arnell. There were three other mobile engineers (as those in charge of recording cars were designated), all veterans of wartime broadcasting in the field, whom I worked with frequently during this period with the European Service. There was Harvey Sarney, a tall, rather saturnine, somewhat lugubrious man with a cadaverous figure, who was never surprised at anything; there was John 'Viz' Vizard who was one of the great bluffers of this world; and there was Stanley Unwin, a wise-cracking humourist, speaking that curious language of his own which perhaps I could call 'Frunwin'.

Stanley and I got on well and I think I was the first to give him a chance to show off his paces on the air when I recorded a spoof interview, in which I as the earnest enquirer was trying to elicit information from Professor Stanley Unwin on some pseudo philosophical subject. I seem to remember arranging for the result to be broadcast, though in what programme I cannot recall. It was not long after that Stanley began to be in demand and was very popular with producers of both radio and TV for a five-minute fill-in.

Amongst those I interviewed more seriously were Peter Scott, the artist and naturalist, who broadcast frequent pieces for us on sailing and whom later I saw at his bird sanctuary home in Gloucester; and Hugh Casson, a future president of the Royal Academy. He was an excellent interview subject and also had great

71

patience. His slightly impish, quizzical look reminded me very much of the famous Fougasse drawings in *Punch*, characters who always had up-tilted noses.

One out of the way character whom I also interviewed was Bert Cozens, one of the first people to do the sort of mad marathon things that nowadays so many achieve for the sake of getting into the *Guinness Book of Records*. He was walking from John-O-Groats, I think it was, down through the length of England and was to continue walking on the Queen Mary, across the Atlantic and on across the States. He was walking when I caught up with him at Wembley, round and round the stadium, and I suddenly had the idea of listening to his heartbeat, using the microphone as a stethoscope. The effect was like that of a steady ship's engine and, heard for the first time, was quite dramatic.

Amongst the foreign language commentators who were part of the 'circus' for which I was sometimes ringmaster, were Messieurs Simon, a vast, cheerful Belgian with tremendous wit which could sometimes be acerbic; Belfer, a typical Frenchman who spoke with rapid fire and gesticulated embellishment; Charles Ricono of the Italian Service, one of the most charming men I have ever met and such a pleasure to work with; and Bill Greenslade, one of the presentation announcers who read the news in English as well as introducing programmes. Bill later joined 'Home Presentation' to do the same job at Broadcasting House.

Then there was George Mikes of the Hungarian Service. George had a wicked, mercurial wit and achieved immediate notoriety when he wrote the super little book called *How To Be An Alien*. It was one of the best-sellers of the day and I treasure my copy with his inscription in it. His follow-up on America entitled *How To Scrape Skies*, did not, as so often happens with a sequel, quite live up to the original. George was tremendous fun to be with and there was always laughter around him.

The 'Britain Can Make It' Exhibition, at which I had done a record number of interviews, was the brainchild of James Gardner. Though at the time extremely busy with the finishing touches (exhibitions always open unfinished) James could not have shown me greater courtesy or co-operation and gave me a brilliant interview or two. I was so glad to hear him on the air only the other day, explaining how his firm were exporting designs and earning foreign currency around the world. At seventy-eight he appears to be going very strong.

I've mentioned Konrad Syrop. His boss, who took over from Gibson Parker (Gibson had just got a very prestigious new appointment as director of programmes for the United Nations radio), was George Camacho. George, as his name might imply, was of Latin American origin and swarthy of appearance with a twinkling face and hair *en brosse*, the overall affect being that of an animated, friendly, koala bear, his button-like eyes enhancing the similarity. He was a very kind and generous man, though he expected a high standard from his subordinates. He was not awe-inspiring like Lobby and you did your best for him for different reasons. He was always very co-operative in helping me to further my career by allowing me time off from any European work, such as at Wimbledon in 1948, to do anything that the domestic services requested. I was always very grateful to George.

On one occasion I took the 'circus' to board the Queen Elizabeth on her first voyage, when recommissioned after her war-time service. Joining the ship at the same time was the Russian delegation to the United Nations, with the famous Foreign Minister, Mr Molotov, at its head. Like Bernard Shaw Mr Molotov was known for never giving an interview, so naturally I had to have a go. I stationed myself at the head of the gangway, where he could not possibly pass me without my getting in a question. As he and his bodyguards hastened up I stepped forward, thrust the microphone in front of him and said 'Would you please say something for the British public, Mr Molotov'. Back like a sniper's bullet came the famous '*Niet!*' and he swept on with his retinue. Well . . . I had tried! Shades of Bernard Shaw. My next downfall was to be at the hands of Walt Disney.

I have always been an innocent, liable to swallow anything said with a straight face. So I was natural meat for someone like Walt Disney, had I but realised it. He was appearing at the Empress Hall, Earls Court and I was sent to interview him backstage. Eventually I found him and he readily agreed to my request for an interview. Having started, he suddenly turned to a companion standing with him saying, 'Oh by the way, this is my friend, the Bishop of Timbuctoo, I'm sure you would like to have an opinion from him'. Somewhat taken aback but completely unsuspecting, I politely turned to the 'Bishop'. I forget what the subject of the interview was but he gave me a very serious answer to my question and continued in what became almost a monologue. I began to get rather annoyed, for I was there to interview Walt Disney. I eventually managed to cut him short and turned back to the great man. 'As you were saying, Mr Disney,' I prompted him, but again he turned to his friend and said 'I'm sure the Bishop will answer that much better'. By this time light was beginning to dawn in even my feeble mind and after a somewhat rueful laugh I managed to get an interview from Disney.

One of the big programmes in a series on the Marshall Plan, called *The Road to Recovery*, concerned the British motor industry and the 'circus' found itself visiting Ford's to do a series of interviews and commentaries on the various processes involved. The head of public relations was Colonel Maurice Buckmaster, who had been in command of the famous Baker Street mob which had controlled allied agents in occupied France during the war. I was sorry not to be able to question him about that also. It would have been a lot more interesting than what was, in the final analysis, little more than a commercial 'spiel'.

Looking through my diaries of the day of that period I am amazed at the variety and number of events that I was involved in, either as commentator or producer or sometimes both. How one managed to get so much in I can't think, for I was regularly doing at least two jobs in one day (and sometimes even three) at often widely separate venues. I'm sure that it must be a reflection of the fact that, not only were the events themselves simpler and often did not involve so many people – in those early days of television Outside Broadcasts everything was 'live', and less time was taken up with the paraphernalia of it all – but also that it was so much easier to get across London from venue to venue. The volume of traffic must have been a tenth of what it is now.

A glance at the headings of the things that I was covering – one moment boxing; the next winter sports; followed by childrens' TV at Chessington Zoo; squash; motor-racing; official visits of foreign Royalty; The International Hotel Congress; The Business Efficiency Exhibition; The Building Trades Exhibition; the return of the Sadlers Wells Ballet from a foreign trip; the Bertram Mills Christmas Circus; the Christmas tree annually presented and set up in Trafalgar Square by a grateful Norwegian Nation; Party Conferences; and interviews with all and sundry in sport or otherwise, including the 'Fluffers', the good ladies who daily cleaned the Underground system in the small hours – gives some indication of that tremendous variety.

During this period I was being increasingly used by Home and

Light programmes, no doubt under the influence of Lobby, who was probably trying me out in different roles. Somebody had had the brainwave of doing a complete hour of boxing from four different venues, under the title 'Four Rings Boxing'. This meant calling on relatively untried boxing commentators, since the number one, Stewart MacPherson, could not be in four places at once. My job was to go to Wisbech where there was a bill of six bouts, varying between four and eight rounds each – all between little-known boxers. For the sake of having a result, one of the four-round bouts was chosen for our contribution to the 'Four Rings' broadcast.

I prepared myself minutely with background information as to the two contestants and also, for the sake of insurance, with the two boxers in the following bout. So, imagine my consternation when, as they cued over to me just after the fight had begun and I had started on my prepared introduction, 'From Wisbech in the heart of jam country', my 'anguished eye' suddenly became aware of one man prone on the canvas and the referee's voice intoning 'four . . . five . . . six'. I barely managed to name the two boxers before the flattened one was counted out and our chosen bout was at an end. Never mind, I thought to myself, thank goodness I prepared the next one – as hurriedly two more men were hustled into the ring. I was just starting to name them when some sixth sense made me glance at Barrington Dalby, a marvellous character and a famous summariser at that time who was sitting beside me. Barry, who had a natural flutter in one eye, was looking rather more excited than usual. His yardarm was ablaze with urgent signals and his head was shaking vigorously. Covering my lip-mike, I hissed 'What's up?' 'Wrong bout!' said Barry.

While I was bluffing my way around my introducion to the next match, Barry feverishly made sure of the identities of the two protagonists. Indeed, they were not the bout in the printed programme at all but a pair quickly substituted by the organisers who, after the débacle of the first fight, had decided that these two would make a far better match for us to describe. I learned a lesson that day – that one always needed to be fully prepared with as much information as possible to cover any eventuality. Richard Dimbleby was the arch exponent of this. He always had an amazing flow of information, which he would deliver – without any hint of apprehension – when things were going wrong. His audience would have no idea that anything untoward was happening.

75

Reverting to Barry Dalby. He was an excellent summariser, renowned for his knowledge of boxing, having been a highly respected international referee. In the days when he was paired with Raymond Glendenning, Stewart MacPherson or Eamonn Andrews, 'Come in, Barry' was a catchphrase that everyone knew. But he was also a very ardent Wimbledon fan. Every year I used to see him sitting in the middle of the front row of the open seats at the side of the court diagonally opposite our box, a knotted hand-kerchief giving slight protection to his head as it swivelled to and fro like a predictor-operated twin Oerlikon locked onto a low-flowing aircraft, one eyelid fluttering animatedly with each stroke. He was a wholehearted enthusiast and a kindly man in everything he did.

When the first postwar British motor-racing Grand Prix was held at Silverstone in 1948, I found myself – somewhat to my surprise – chosen to do the commentary. True, there was no-one obvious in sight at the time and Lobby presumably thought that if I had the speed for Wimbledon I should be all right for motor-racing. Nothing could really have been further from the truth. Though I love driving a good car, I am completely unmechanical, totally untechnical, hate noise, and find the fumes generated by a pack of racing cars quite unpalatable. I did my best and as a result, before there was too much protest and I was fully found out, I actually covered some five races. One of those was the Jersey Grand Prix, where I was stationed behind a low stone wall in a private garden at the apex of a hairpin bend. The thought did occur to me that I was not in the best of positions if somebody came down the approach too fast, failed to make the turn and drifted out across the road. Indeed one did and I was glad of the stone wall.

My *coup de grâce* followed a spoonerism – quite harmless in normal circles – but not to the unforgiving closed ranks of the motor-racing fraternity. In my excitement, as one of the leaders streaked by in the second Silverstone Grand Prix that I covered, I yelled, 'There goes Ferrari in a Farina'. I had gone too far and, though my pride was dented, I was really very relieved when Raymond Baxter, a Spitfire pilot and very much a vroom . . . vroom man, was brought in to take over.

Despite this I found myself still in increasing demand, not only for radio outside broadcasts but for the newly burgeoning activities of television. There was in those days no recording of TV, so that every programme was live. This meant that commentators and 'in vision' presenters, who could be depended upon to live up to Kipling and keep going in what sometimes were the wildest and most bewildering of circumstances, were quite at a premium. This was all the more so, since nearly all the producers and directors were beginners themselves, most of whom had come from radio.

When things were going wrong the wretched presenter/interviewer was frequently the last to know about it. Sometimes in these situations you felt totally exposed, marooned like a forgotten man on an atom-test atoll, or like the boy who 'stood on the burning deck, whence all but he had fled'. You were rooted in front of the camera when perhaps it or the microphone – or both – had 'gone down', trying to decipher signals from the stage manager, who was in headphone contact with the producer in the OB van. Some of the of the 'live' situations in the early days were indescribable. Strong men wilted and sometimes only recovered their poise and sense of humour in the post-programme sanctuary of the bar. I remember once seeing the camera apparently being dismantled before my very eyes but still having to obey the gesticulations of the SM to keep going, while the camera's red light glowed like an unblinking basilisk, indicating that it was on transmission.

One man I did a lot of work with in those days was Berkeley Smith. His chain smoking increased in tempo with the advent of each new complication of a television OB. His instructions would become terser and terser, being punctuated by puff . . . puff . . . puff. One particularly fraught OB that he was in charge of was at the Empire Pool at Wembley where the famous Harlem Globetrotters, the greatest basketball players in the world at that time, were playing a demonstration match. My role in this was to do some half-time interviews – in particular with their star shooter, and it had been arranged that these would also be 'fed' on the public address system so that the watching crowd could hear them and not get restless. Berkeley's assistant or stage manager was a marvellous character called Steve Wade, whose eyes were always glinting mischievously through his glasses and whose wiry hair tended to stand up and look like a sweep's brush. Steve could always be relied upon to come up with at least six different courses of action to take in any given crisis. He was the arch-improviser in what in the circumstances was always a band of improvisers.

I was 'on my marks' on the touchline, for Berkeley's latest hissed instruction, puff, puff, puff, to me had been 'Max' . . . puff . . .

'When the half-time whistle goes' . . . puff . . . puff . . . 'I want you to get right out there' . . . puff . . . puff . . . puff 'as fast as you can' . . . puff. With this injunction in my mind I was off like a flash as soon as the whistle went, stationing myself on the agreed mark alongside the globetrotting hero. He was immense, towering above me, and I was getting almost a crick in my neck as I started on my interview. Suddenly I became aware that the whole of the Empire Pool audience was laughing. For me the interview was deadly serious and I could not think what could be so funny, though I thought I could discern an amused glint in the giant's eye. However, I gallantly ploughed on while the laughter turned into a gale. I was getting desperate but still kept going. I have always had good peripheral vision and suddenly became aware out of the corner of my right eye (don't forget I was looking up at my giant friend) of what seemed to be a large snake writhing on the floor. Just as I was wondering what best to do, I felt an object being thrust into my hand. Steve Wade had come to the rescue, sliding along the ground to keep out of camera vision, and had brought me – my microphone!

Berkeley was to suffer with me once more when I was doing what became an annual event with him, the Royal Tournament at Olympia. I stress again that in those days everything was 'live' and there was no going back. My job on this occasion was to interview an RAF dog handler. He was very proud of his Alsatian, whose name was Shandy, and demonstrated the various commands that Shandy obeyed instantly. Having got him to 'sit!', he asked me whether I would like to have a go. I, of course, said 'yes'. After all these revelations I feel I shall be known as the Spoonerism King, for the command that I gave in ringing tones was 'Sandy – shit!' I nearly did myself! Fortunately, Shandy remained unmoved.

Berkeley, Steve and I did many jobs together. Both had long and distinguished service in television as OB producers, Berkeley also doing a lot of presenting. He became Controller of Programmes in Southern Television and ended his service in the very important job of co-ordinating the programme councils of the various ITV companies. Steve at the time also had a special job *vis-a-vis* me. This was to distract me by his facial contortions as we were about to come on the air, so that my strained serious look should break into a welcoming smile for the viewers.

Meanwhile, life rushed on pleasurably. During 1949 I had been seeing quite a lot of Elisabeth Beresford, the girl who had looked after me at Brighton. We arranged to go and stay a week in Amsterdam with Hans van Swol, the Dutch tennis player who had been saved on the Centre Court by the squirrel, and his delightful English wife, Valerie, both of whom I had got to know when they had just become engaged during the postwar Britannia Shield Competition, which involved various sports, between teams from the Allied Nations. While in Amsterdam, I managed to persuade Liza to become engaged and even to agree to a quick wedding. She probably said 'yes', thinking there was no way I could bring it about. Fortunately for me, I had to come back in the middle of that week to co-host *Picture Page* with Joan Gilbert, since her regular colleague, Leslie Mitchell, was unavailable. It was a great chance for me, for it was my first appearance in any important TV studio progamme.

To the amusement of those I was working with, I spent all my spare time on the telephone, arranging a registrar's marriage in Brighton followed by a Blessing Ceremony at St Colomba's Church near Harrods. Having completed these swift arrangements, I returned to Amsterdam triumphant. The press made much of it with the headline 'Eight Day Courtship', which of course it had not been, and as far as I recall I (we – Liza came along too) spent the first day of our honeymoon interviewing the ladies of the Burwash Women's Institute.

9

COMING 'HOME'

D URING MY LAST FEW MONTHS WITH THE EUROPEAN SERVICE I WAS DOING ALMOST AS MUCH WORK FOR THE HOME AND LIGHT programmes and various television outside broadcasts as I was for the European Service itself, as well as doing commentaries for television Newsreel. It was all great experience for what was to come.

Early in 1950 I had put in for the job of a producer in Children's Television, though I had no great hankering after getting it. Then suddenly my horizons widened when Wynford Vaughan-Thomas, one of the best-known staff commentators (whose vivid wartime despatches had endeared him to listeners), decided to go freelance, leaving a vacancy on the establishment of Outside Broadcasts (radio). This was what I really wanted and I put in for it. I realised that there was little hope for me, since it was known on the grapevine that there were two leading candidates. Audrey Russell was reputed to be favoured by Lobby (who had lately been appointed Generalissimo of both television and radio Outside Broadcasts); while Raymond Baxter was said to be the front runner of Charles Max-Muller (who was now, under Lobby, assistant head of Outside Broadcasts (radio)). Fortunately for me the board was being chaired by the appointments officer and one of the junior members of Appointments, a friend of mine, Anthony Craxton, was acting as usher to the candidates. He was a great help in doing his best to put me at my ease.

First we were given a test to do, the orders for which ran as follows.

By way of a practical test you are asked to contribute a 5 minute extempore broadcast to a series within 'Glimpses of London' which is being carried in the General Overseas Service. Your theme will be 'London's Secondhand Car Market' and you should imagine an announcement which reads –

'This week's Glimpse of London takes you to London's principle secondhand car market. Our observer has just left the market in Great Portland Street and is at a microphone in a neighbouring building. We take you over to him now.'

N.B. There is no need to imagine that the microphone is at a window overlooking Great Portland Street.

My knowledge of cars was practically nil, whereas it was very much Raymond's subject. I wondered whose decision this test was! Anyway, I hurried down Great Portland Street, which in those days was full of secondhand car emporia, whose owners or assistants tended to prey from the pavement on passers-by – rather like the street arabs of the Middle East. Each time I started enquiring of one of them some of the facts of the secondhand car business, he naturally thought I might be a buyer and some time was wasted in disabusing him. Gradually I was beginning to get a little information together, but didn't really feel it was taking me very far, when I met a most friendly and helpful soul. His name was Mick Adelston and he really gave me the gen. I think I was helped by the fact that he was an ardent sports fan and probably recognised me already from television.

Armed by Mick with all the information I could assimilate I hastened back to my 'studio' in the Redbourne, which was the office block in which the Board was taking place. Fortunately, doing reports from Wimbledon – and all I had experienced with Angus Mackay – had given me the ability to ad lib pieces to an exact time, which was what was required on this occasion. Then came the board itself – of which I remember very little.

But I do remember going back to Bush House very despondently, feeling that I would not get the job. To my delight a few days later I received a memo from the Appointments Officer saying:

Thank you for coming to the Appointment Board for the O.B. Post on the 3rd March. I am glad to tell you that you have been selected for this vacancy. . .

Anthony later told me that I owed my good fortune partly to the fact that the two leading protagonists had each held their ground for their own candidate and I was the compromise solution. Another factor in my favour was that I had done my secondhand car report ad lib, as the orders had stated, whereas apparently Raymond had prepared a script. However, he was far too good to be left out for long, and fortunately he got the next vacancy, which came up fairly soon.

The change-over to the 'Home' establishment in Outside Broadcasts, although it raised my status, also brought me much more to heel. I was no longer quite the untrammelled agent that I had been in the European Service where, as long as the results were coming in, I had largely been left to my own devices. All of us on the OB establishment were there as producers, although most of us also were used as commentators. It was not long before I found myself being handed out one or two large-scale programmes to devise in concept and select the detail of – programmes like *Roman Road to Canterbury, London Bus Rides, The LCC, Port of London*, etc. Having been given this general theme, which had been agreed at some programme meeting, it was up to the individual producer to get on with it. A pool of subjects for incorporation in the theme might be discussed at a departmental meeting, which we had weekly, or with colleagues who would pitch in with ideas. Gradually an overall picture would emerge and you would then set about prospecting the venues concerned. It was also important to find the right spot from which to do the linking commentary. Obviously for the *London Bus Rides* the moving bus was the threading link. Another time I linked from the gallery running round the outside of the dome of St Paul's. A position like this gave one ready access to lots of landmarks and historical references, which were all good 'associative material' – an essential ingredient of the general construction of an outside broadcast of this type.

Much effort and money was put into these large programmes, which were clearly devised to show the radio flag in as big a way as possible before the inevitable and dreaded onslaught of television, which was bound to take over much of radio's traditional territory. It would still be a while before televison was able to put enough outside broadcast units into the field to cover a wide programme spectrum in this way. However, the Queen's accession and the ceremonies that would follow for a year or two, undoubtedly

82

hastened the proper equipping of TV Outside Broadcasts. The flooding tide of TV success brought despair to the old guard at Broadcasting House. It was gloom and doom in those days. It would have been a brave and inspired prophet who could then have foretold the marvellous comeback that radio would make.

One of the benefits of being a producer in charge of programmes like these, or even smaller scale ones like the State Opening of Parliament, was that one was working with the greats like Richard Dimbleby and Wynford Vaughan-Thomas. In fact such was the respect accorded those two – and awareness of the rivalry thought to exist between them (although I'm pretty sure that was exaggerated) – that by general consent they would be allotted the big parts alternately. They were totally different characters and broadcasters. Richard Dimbleby was *sans pareil* in the majesty and invincibility of his style. His natural slow, measured manner gave him not only more time to think but was also his copyright, although John Arlott had a similar approach to cricket commentary. Both Richard and John in their diverse fields were image-makers of genius and, if anybody else had attempted similar slow rhythms, they would have been accused of aping them. Richard's own natural dignity and marvellous sense of the 'right' word and appropriate metaphor made him the master for the big ceremonial. Wynford, on the other hand, like so many of his Welsh countrymen – but even more than most – had an effervescent, ever-ready flow of words. He literally bubbled and everything was made to sound more entrancing, magical and vitally interesting.

It was because Richard Dimbleby was ill, that on April Fools Day 1950 I did interviews for television at the start of the Boat Race. Rowing has never been a particular interest of mine, but I had enough native curiosity to be able to ask sensible questions and seemed to do all right. As a result I was asked again the following year. This time, instead of being at the start, I was stationed some three-quarters of the way down the course. The idea was that I should do some pre-race interviews with the crowds linking the banks and also be ready to be cued to for a riverside comment as the crews came by.

The first part of my brief went without a hitch; the second did not. During the race, in very gusty and turbulent water conditions, technical trouble with the camera following the race at that moment, forced the producer to come over to me early and unceremoniously, with an urgent shout from the SM to grab someone for interview and keep going till further notice. This I did and was soon intently filibustering with my victim. Meanwhile, the stage manager with me was trying ineffectually to get me to stop and hand back. But he did not get near enough to my eye-line, so that I was quite oblivious of his signals. By this time the producer was suffering from apoplexy and despair. Why? Because they had managed to get the camera going again and the Oxford boat was *sinking*. Remember? I think they got back just in time for the dénouement, but next year needless to say, the boat race took place without the help of innocent blinkered Muggins Max.

All the time I was with OB's I was constantly being called up to Alexandra Palace, which was the home of BBC television in those days, to record commentaries on various sporting events for television Newsreel. The editor of this was Richard Cawston. He was so nice and yet so professional, but I doubt whether he would have gone very far in present day television – he was not nearly ruthless enough. He was to be known later for his documentaries on the royal family, but alas, died early. Working with Dick was a real pleasure. Paul Fox, later editor of *Grandstand* and now Managing Director of Yorkshire T.V., served some of his apprenticeship under Richard Cawston and I am sure learned a lot from him.

Usually I had reasonable notice when Dick wanted me for a job, but I remember one particular day, 5 May 1954, (after I had gone freelance) when I received a very urgent call and rushed up to Ally Pally. The emergency was caused by the fact that this was an historic day for athletics. Almost in secret, but fortunately still covered by a film camera, Roger Bannister, paced first by Chris Brasher and then Chris Chataway, had broken the four-minute mile at Oxford. The film was rushed to Alexandra Palace and I recorded the commentary. The piece went out on the News that night – and has often been used since in look-back progammes.

Early in 1951 I managed to persuade Godfrey Adams, one of the two chief programme planners for radio, that it might be a good idea to break new ground and try doing a commentary on squash. So he, John Snagge and I went down to the Lansdowne Club, just off Berkeley Square, and I had a dummy run during one of the Amateur Championship matches. They decided it was worth having a go, so next year we did it – the first time it was ever attempted, I believe. It was a very difficult thing to do, as anyone who understands squash will realise. The rallies are long and there is

84

very little time between each stroke. If you try to follow each shot it can soon become extremely boring. If, on the other hand, you start reading the pattern of the rally, it is ten to one that a player suddenly makes a winning coup and you have missed it. On the whole, although we did do it for a couple of years more, it was not really a success.

But despite the occasional disappointment or hiccup, these were great years. If I felt I had been an all-rounder with the European Service, I became even more so with OBs. Those were the days when radio Outside Broadcasts were still relatively in their infancy and television was learning with every experience. There was no money in television, or very little for any freelance, so that the big agents and top journalists were not yet into it. It was all so new that the one or two people who could be relied on were in demand for pretty well everything and, as I was SNF (Staff-No-Fee), I was hauled in for all manner of different subjects. It was a super job to have at a time that for most British was grey, comfortless and, after the deprivations of the war, rather hopeless. Instead of life improving it seemed to be getting worse. But for me, the excitement of new worlds opening up almost daily brought intense satisfaction and made it a time of sheer romance.

10

STATE OCCASIONS

O NE OF THE MOST UNFORGETTABLE OCCASIONS THAT I COVERED FOR OUTSIDE BROADCASTS – NOT ON MY OWN, BUT AS NUMBER two to Wynford Vaughan-Thomas – took place in Westminster Hall. It was a double celebration: the 900th Anniversary of this ancient building that was so integral a part of our national heritage and the opening of the new House of Commons Chamber, rebuilt after having been blitzed during the war. It was a tremendous occasion, and Wynford did his stuff magnificently, his glittering phrases keeping pace with the fanfares of the trumpets. When the royal procession was nearing its majestic end, just before the entry of the Queen Mother, Wynford almost sang her introduction with the immortal words, 'The trumpets shrill! The doors are flung wide! And there enters that most gracious, that most loved figure, His Majesty . . . Queen Mary.' Wynford, fortunately, was blissfully unaware of his bloomer and was now in full swing, describing the entry of the King and Queen. It was too late to go back and in any event it would have been dreadful to have done so. I held my peace.

I know only too well how easy it is to commit gaffes of this sort. Unfortunately they then become immortalised. On the occasion of the official visit of the King and Queen of Denmark, the usual fixed protocol engagements for such an event included a formal drive to Guildhall for a luncheon given by the Lord Mayor. This time I was the commentator at Guildhall for radio. These occasions were always nervous ones, because rightly or wrongly one always felt they were listened to more keenly by authority; for in those days the awe and reverence that used to surround royalty was still very much in evidence.

With Christine Janes in our Centre Court position 1986. Listeners seemed to enjoy our Mixed Doubles matches on Radio 2.

Interviewing Ann Jones after she won the Wimbledon title in 1969.

The author: *above*, at 12½ months; *right*, at 9 and *below*, at pre-prep school in Winchester. As wicket-keeper in the Summer of 1924, I was an old colour (right of the four). Second from the left is N.S. Mitchell-Innes, who captained England after the war.

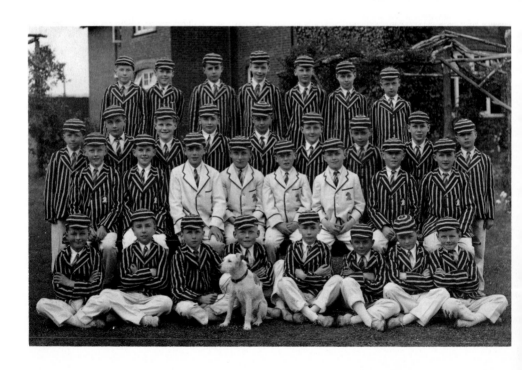

Left, Upper Cassowary Camp, scene of the reticulated python encounter. My beard was reddish and very apostolic!

Above, Fidlin panning the concentrates of a clean-up from the boxes which had been mixed with mercury to pick up the colours and form a gold amalgam. Periodically the amalgam would be retorted and the residual almost pure gold sent to the bank for assay.

The river has been dammed. The 'wash', cleared of the 'overburden', was put through the boxes. The heavy gold was caught in cane 'riffles'. The boxes were regularly 'cleaned up' and the concentrates dealt with as above.

Princess Elizabeth's wedding 20 November 1947. The royal carriage entering the Mall on returning from Westminster Abbey. I was commentating for the European Service from the roof of the Admiralty stronghold.

Nancy (Suttor), my first wife, in the garden of our flat in New Farm, Brisbane, 1938.

Tinker–Tailor, the M.O.I. Film of the Maritime Royal Artillery, being shot at Pinewood during the war. Director Alex Shaw has a technical point for me.

Above, 'Lobby' Seymour de Lotbiniere, listening to Carl Erhardt (Ice-Hockey Association) at a pre-Olympic get-together. Everyone 'looked up' to Lobby.

L–R, Lord Brabazon (President of the Cresta), M.R., Sir Arnold Lunn (the father of Alpine Ski-ing), 'Tyke' Richardson (*The Times* Skating Correspondent), Carl Erhardt (Chairman of the Ice-Hockey Association).

George Bernard Shaw just before his ninetieth birthday. When he broke a leg, the BBC (Yours apprehensively) was summoned to his bedside to record his speech of thanks to the St. Pancras Council, who were giving him the freedom of the borough.

BBC

Harold Abrahams (centre) and Rex Alston (right) with the author at the 1948 London Olympics.

The Princess Elizabeth inspects the guard of honour of ex-servicemen, on her arrival at St. John's Newfoundland before boarding the 'Empress of Scotland' at the end of the royal tour of Canada, Autumn 1951.

1948 Pre-Olympic Training of European Service commentators. 'Eddie' (Olive Edmonds), my secretary, projecting Leni Riefenstahl's films of the 1936 Winter Olympics at Garmisch Partenkirchen. Charles Ricono of the Italian Service was being put through his paces by me.

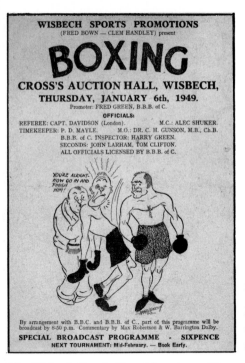

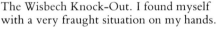

The Wisbech Knock-Out. I found myself with a very fraught situation on my hands.

A Nicer Knock-Out. Liza (Elisabeth Beresford) before we married.

The Announcers' Room at Broadcasting House in 1951. L-R. Alan Skempton, Colin Doran, Alvar Liddell, Lionel Marson, Robin Holmes, Bob Dougal and Frank Phillips. Television was still only a small cloud on their horizon.

The Royal Tour of Canada, 1951.

Above, an Unlikely Tale. John Snagge (left), experienced fisherman, with nary a bite and yours truly, 'compleat' beginner, with a Coho salmon. Caught in Cowichan Bay, Vancouver Island.

Left, Corey Thompson a Canadian reporter on the Royal Tour. He asked the Duke of Edinburgh for a 'contribution' and got less than he hoped.

The Coronation Fleet Review, June 1953.

Representing Italy, the training vessel 'Amerigo Vespucci', her shrouds fully manned.

Sir Winston looks wistful as he surveys the last great gathering of Britain's conventional sea power.

The Prime Minister, Sir Winston Churchill, on board the Trinity House Vessel, Patricia, reads a signal from the Duke of Gloucester, the titular Master of Trinity House. Looking on were Christopher Soames (left) and Captain Gerald Curteis, the Deputy Master and executive head.

Waiting to go on the air and very aware of 'a certain naval person' in earshot.

Panorama in Rome. Richard Dimbleby interviews Sophia Loren.

Ronnie Noble and Peter Dimmock –
Cortina, 1956 Winter Olympics.

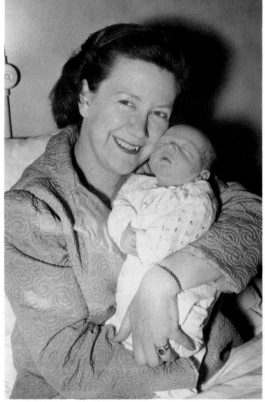

'Introducing Marcus' was the *Daily
Mail's* back page caption for the
Monday after the Cortina Winter
Olympics.

Panorama pioneers. L–R. M.R., the Rt. Hon. Jack Ashley M.P. and the originator and first editor of the programme, Andrew Miller-Jones – celebrating twenty years on.

Benny Hill, Terry Thomas and Tony Hancock don't seem at all happy.

Kitty or 'Biddy' Godfree, Wimbledon Champion in 1924 and 1926, with the portrait of her when she won her first title. I had discovered it in a junk shop.

'Willie Woodworm' goes to work on a piece. It was always fascinating to follow his knowledge and expertise.

John Gaisford

'Game Ball' is the title of this watercolour, dated 25th April 1877, two months before the first Wimbledon championships. It is the earliest known painting of a lawn tennis player.

John Gaisford

Dated 1884, this parian figure is probably of William Renshaw who won Wimbledon for the fourth time running that year.

The first bit of Chinese porcelain I bought that was 'right'. It cost me £4.10 nearly thirty years ago.

John Gaisford

The Nanking Cargo.

Where Every Prospect Pleases.

Mike Hatcher and friends.

Mike Hatcher – the Cousteau of Salvage

John Gaisford

Top right, a very rare cat night-light from the cargo of a mid 17th century junk, which was Hatcher's first salvage of Chinese porcelain. This porcelain was auctioned in three sales by Christie's (Amsterdam) in 1984–85.

A unique group of superb quality small vases, all clearly painted by the same hand – also from the junk.

Sterling courage and stamina were needed if the 168,000 pieces of the Nanking cargo, sold for a total of £10,000,000, were to be properly viewed. In fact, with the best will in the world, it was an impossible task.

Palm Springs, 1978. The sun is setting fast for British hopes in the Davis Cup Final. L-R. M.R., Dan Maskell, Gerry Williams, Geoff Dobson. The engineers seem to have a very mixed outlook on the subject.

Above, working with director, Bob Evans (right) on a series for Channel 4 to be shown in 1987. Each programme featured a Sotheby expert on his specialised subject.

Sporting line-up to cut the red tape and open Haileybury's new Sports Hall, November 1986. R-L. Rugby International, Peter Warfield; ex World water-ski jumping champion, Paul Seaton; Alan Fairbairn (Amateur Squash Champion 1953, 1954); Stirling Moss; and M.R. – all old

Once inside Guildhall at my vantage point in the gallery, I applied myself to getting ready for the description of the magnificent banquet scene below me. Being very nervous I did what I seldom did on an outside broadcast (unless very frightened) – I wrote an introduction which gave an overall short description. After this I ad libbed, identifying the personages present, starting from the ends of the table. Everything seemed to be going quite well and I was gathering confidence as I reached the most important figures at the centre, until finally I came to Queen Ingrid, whom I described as 'looking absolutely beautiful . . . wearing an off-the-hat face'. Those words will follow me to my broadcasting grave.

Two other near disastrous occasions I am reminded of both happened in Paris. They were wonderful illustrations of just how haphazard covering anything under the aegis of French radio or television was then liable to be. In one of them I was to describe for the European Service the ceremony of the 'Sixteen Nations' signing of the European Pact. It was in a magnificent but small chamber at the Quai d'Orsay – the French Foreign Office. The chairman of the Signing Ceremony was the Foreign Secretary – Ernest Bevin – one of the greatest figures ever of the British Labour Party. I had a position in a corner of the room between the entrance door and a window. Zero hour was approaching and I suddenly realised I had no microphone. The chairman was already rapping the table, throats were being cleared, silence was descending, and I was as desperate as any man can be, when suddenly a hand came through the window and gave me my microphone. Simultaneously another disembodied hand cued me that I was on the air. And so – miraculously – I was!

On a like occasion at the Champs Elysées Wynford was waiting, preparing himself to do a commentary on some great French Remembrance parade. He was having the same trouble as I had experienced. Listeners down the rehearsal line before he came on the air heard an unrecognisable Wynford, almost sobbing his entreaties as he talked to the local BBC representative in the Paris studio. 'Cecile', he lamented, 'Cecile, there's no microphone, they've given me no microphone'. There was a moment's pause followed by a distant fanfare and then in Wynford's best ceremonial manner, his voice as firm as ever, came over something like 'And now as the head of the parade swings around the Arc. . .' Obviously a last minute hand had appeared for him also.

STOP TALKING AND GIVE THE SCORE

Another overseas trip I will never forget was the royal tour of Canada in the autumn of 1951. I think it was probably due to the support of Godfrey Adams – an austere man who did not easily show any feelings, but with whom I felt I had developed some slight bond – that I was chosen to cover this event with John Snagge and Godfrey Talbot. King George was not well enough to go and instead Princess Elizabeth and the Duke of Edinburgh were deputising for him. It was to be something of a whistle-stop tour, with little time at each venue, except the very big centres like Quebec and Toronto. Godfrey was to be with the press corps immediately in attendance on the royal party, while John and I had the job of leap-frogging across Canada a few days ahead of the royal entourage. Our brief was to bring to listeners back at home what we were seeing through British eyes and so, it was hoped, give an appreciation of what the royal couple would be feeling.

Meanwhile the press corps, travelling with the royal party, included one of the most popular of all Canadian reporters, Corey Thompson. He was a cheerful and resourceful soul, who had no experience of royal protocol and apparently little regard for it. The first time that he found himself in the royal retinue, he sidled up to the Duke of Edinburgh and, thrusting a microphone before him, said, 'Say, Dook, won't you say a few words for us?' The Duke's form of *Niet!* was to put his hand in his trouser pocket, extract a coin and place it on the upturned face of the microphone. Quite unabashed, at the next possible chance, Corey again presented his microphone – this time with the entreaty, 'Say, Dook, may I have a contribution *now*?' And this time the 'mike' face had a slot in it.

For John and me it was a frantic experience. We would have literally only twenty four hours to arrive at a place, make the necessary contacts with the local Radio Station, set about recommended interviews or short recorded commentaries at points of interest, record a report or two and take the whole package to the Studios for transmission back to England where various uses would be made of it. Then sleep was the next priority – often a catnap – and on again some hundreds of miles to the next venue.

John and I saw each other at only three points on the trip. I was the first to arrive and covered Quebec – suddenly becoming aware of the intensely national French feeling, which hadn't at that stage made itself obvious at an international level. I saw John very briefly in Toronto – in fact so briefly that I had to consult him while he was having a bath – and then it was off again. The next time we met was at the extremity of the tour, Vancouver Island in British Columbia. By then, even though in those days I had masses of energy, I was really feeling the effects and was only too anxious, after a day of recording mainly ancient Indian songs, to get to bed and have a long recuperative sleep.

Alas, for my hopes. John Snagge was known to be a mad keen fisherman and it transpired that 'Ches' Chesnut, the local Radio Station Manager, was also a fishing fiend. They were determined to catch salmon and equally determined that I should accompany them at something like 5.30 am. So, protesting loudly and completely bleary-eyed, I suffered them to take me trolling for Coho salmon in Cowichan Bay. I have never felt less inspired in my life. As I'd always understood was the case with fishing, nothing happened. We trolled and we trolled and I was getting colder and more miserable by the minute. Just as I was putting on my mackintosh, and had one arm in and the other half in, I heard a yell from John. A fish had taken my bait. He was just in time to seize the rod before it fell over the edge, and hooked the fish firmly. After that I was given the somewhat empty honour of reeling it in and, as I had never caught a salmon before, was promptly 'blooded' by them. Needless to say, it was the only fish taken that morning. Fate is ironic, for I would have swapped it for sleep any day.

Obviously a tour like this was a tremendous experience and I was constantly seeing and learning new things about people. One thing that struck my forcibly at the time was that everybody was eager to work and get ahead. Nobody minded competition. It was very much the North American feeling.

Vancouver Island was the turning-point of our scamper across the continent and back. John and I did not meet up again until we joined the *Empress of Scotland* at New Brunswick for the return trip. She was also carrying the Princess and Duke back. The Duke had not long before become the president and the twelfth man of the Lord's Taverners, whom I might advisedly call a 'boddey' to promote fellowship in watching cricket beside the Tavern at Lord's with a glass of beer in the hand, while at the same time raising money for National Playing Fields. It was all the brainchild of Martin Boddey, the founder; and, since he was an actor and many of his friends were in the entertainment business, it was like souls who were invited to be the original members. It was a great idea and spread like wildfire, though it was originally supposed to be limited to two hundred members, and the lists had now been closed.

As well as the Duke and John Snagge, who was now chairman and one of the original members, the Duke's equerry, Lieutenant Commander Michael Parker, was also a Taverner. He and John conceived the idea that it would be nice to have a Taverners' four at deck tennis, to be reported back to the committee. As a result I was hastily made a member and the four took place. To begin with it was not taken very seriously, so that John and I managed to win the first game narrowly, but there was no question about the outcome! After this we were privileged to have drinks with the Princess and I was tremendously struck, not only by her delightful sense of humour but also by her sense of duty. For it was she who ensured, when a signal was received from the escorting destroyer joining us off Ireland, that a suitable reply was made.

After their arduous tour Princess Elizabeth and the Duke were having a well-earned holiday in Kenya and the extraordinary experience of a night in 'Treetops', when the news was brought to the new Queen that her father had died on 5 February 1952. So started her long and illustrious reign, with the duties she had just been performing in Canada nothing to those she would·now face. In the next year the ceremonies leading up to the Coronation in 1953 were legion. A by-product was that television Outside Broadcasts really came into its own.

The whole nation sorrowed at the death of King George VI. It was a kingship he had not sought and, with his natural shyness and slight speech impediment, he had found it very difficult. However, brought up to duty, he had accepted the burden and had proved to be a Sovereign – and with Queen Elizabeth beside him – a partnership beloved by all. She was ever a tremendous stay to him. I always remember the first instance of this, of which I was aware. In 1932 a magnificent new dining-hall was built at Haileybury to the plans of Sir Herbert Baker. It really was and has remained a splendid building and one in which young boys are helped unconsciously by, not just the splendour of their surroundings but also a certain homeliness going with it, to acquire the inbred qualities that make for good citizens.

The Duke of York accepted the invitation to open it and I was one of the guard of honour from the school corps provided for the occasion, and drawn up in the quadrangle before the steps from which the Duke would speak. This meant that I was in a very good position in front of him and his radiant Duchess as he declared the building open. There was then a pause . . . that became an awkward pause . . . that seemed to stretch into eternity . . . as all the school including the 'beaks' – they more than any perhaps – waited anxiously for what they had been told would be coming next. Just as the interminable wait was becoming a crisis, the smiling Duchess leaned up and whispered in her husband's ear. He smiled too, and said, 'I believe I also have to ask for a half-holiday'. The relief was so great that the cheers rang out even more loudly.

And in this vein the Queen so often thoughout their reign had supported her husband. All these thoughts were being felt by the silent crowd gathered outside Buckingham Palace in mute tribute and grief and I – on behalf of the General Overseas Service was given the very moving job of doing a five minute account and expression of what they were feeling. They were thinking not only of a loved King who had served them so well, but of the mantle that had fallen prematurely on such young shoulders. There was a marvellous sense of national unison and support for the new Queen – and for what many optimists hoped would be another glorious Elizabethan era.

A few days later I was at Temple Bar for television to witness and describe the scene of the Proclamation of the Queen's Accession as exemplified by the tradition of entering the City with the Lord Mayor's acceptance. It was a very moving ceremony, as I described in my commentary at the time:

> My Lord Mayor presents the pearl sword, gifted to the City by Queen Elizabeth I, to the Sovereign in homage, hilt first, acknowledging homage to the Sovereign. The Queen touches it and returns it to the City, acknowledging that the Sovereign has asked permission to enter the confines of the City.

It was very brief, the procession only stopping for this traditional act, that is so much a part of our history, before going on to Guildhall. I had done as much as I could to prepare myself with 'associative material' by talking to some of the crowd gathered there, in case I had to fill in time. It was just as well I had for the Queen's carriage took some fourteen minutes to reach Temple Bar after I had come on the air. So I was able to talk of one or two of the individuals who had come up in the early hours of the morning to get good places to view the occasion. One was a schoolboy with a wide-striped muffler in his school colours. He was just getting over chicken pox and had no right to be there. Another was a merchant seaman. I also mentioned the dog that ran out into the road and

91

snapped at the horses hooves when the procession moved off. I was hoping to establish the atmosphere – to share it with the listening public – and to show the human face of the crowd.

Unfortunately, one rarely pleases everyone, and later when the programme was reviewed, Peter Dimmock who was television's assistant head of Outside Broadcasts expressed general displeasure, and said that the sort of details I had given were not really suitable for such a ceremonial occasion. However, a little later, the *Listener* wrote in their 'Critic on the Hearth' column:

> The transmission from Temple Bar, where ancient additional ritual imposed itself on the proceedings, was particularly effective, the more so for the excellence of Max Robertson's commentary technique. He had the wit to pick out sympathetic focal points . . . he also realised that we victims of monochrome television were hungry for the colour splendours of the scene and it is a pointer to the future that his generous attempts to minister to this need made us the more so. His was one of the best discharged commentary assignments we have heard on television.

This did much to restore my confidence, and I was grateful to the 'human face' behind the pen.

Members of the public frequently remark that a roving reporter's life, such as mine, must be very pleasant, witnessing – from the best seats – history in the making. But it's also a job like any other job, and every time you go on the air there is the knowledge that you are immediately subjected, not only to the judgment of your bosses but also of the thousands – possibly millions – of listeners. Sometimes this can be nerve-wracking.

My worst experience may possibly have been at the Coronation, the televising of which outstripped anything that had gone before. All the fast-growing resources of Outside Broadcasts were deployed. The planning, under the overall direction of Lobby, was meticulous and the result brilliant on both radio and television. This rarest and most exotic butterfly of pageantry was finely captured by the cameras, still only in black and white, with the rich tapestry of its colours so vividly evoked by the commentary teams led by Richard Dimbleby and Wynford Vaughan-Thomas.

I was with television this time. My position was on the Embankment, where the procession swept past at the trot in a rippling flame of brûlé colour – costumes, plumes and uniforms. It was all over in four and a half minutes during which I was gasping and scrabbling for words and names. It was a nightmare! My producer was one of the most experienced by now – and certainly one of the most artistic, Anthony Craxton. He loved a close-up and was punching up a quick succession of resplendent warriors, debonair courtiers and dignified diplomats from all parts of the world. As each new face appeared there came Anthony's behest 'Identify!' Because of the speed he could not hold a close-up for long and, just as I felt I had found one figure in the order of procession, he cut to his next fancy, who of course would be some way on in the order. His command of 'Identify!' became more exigent as I failed to respond, or at the best was only able lamely to say, 'That was . . .' after the picture had gone. I've never been under so much pressure or felt so frustrated. In my ears was the repeated 'Identify!' 'Widen your shot!' I silently and desperately rejoined, for then I would have had a chance of orientating myself in the ever-flowing cascade of pomp and ceremony.

I have never dared to view and listen to that excerpt since. I received a very nice letter from Lobby afterwards, but I suspect it was a round robin of congratulation on what was overall a fantastic achievement. I was getting some reflected glory that I certainly did not deserve.

Perhaps the most important example of a mammoth outside broadcast that I had to organise was the Coronation Fleet Review in June 1953. It needed a lot of planning and close contact with naval sources, but especially with Trinity House, which is the head-quarters and organising authority for all Britain's lighthouses. At first sight this may seem odd. The reason is that by ancient custom, in any Fleet Review, the reviewing vessels are led out by one from Trinity House. Presumably this was started as a precaution, so that the experts could deal with any obstruction or dangers to the vessels following which carried many important personages.

In this case the Trinity House vessel was their flagship, *Patricia*, and she seemed the ideal floating platform for the linking commentary to be performed from. I had given myself this job, since I felt I had the whole operation more at my fingertips than any of the other commentators, having dealt with every aspect of it from the beginning. I had to liaise with the deputy master of Trinity House who was its true executive officer, the master being a titular position held by the Duke of Gloucester. The deputy master's name was Captain Gerald Curteis, (later Sir Gerald) a most delightful and charming man of the old school. He was courtesy itself and gave me every possible help, gladly allowing me to have our commentary position on the aft poop-deck, so that I would have a perfect view of the destroyer astern of us, carrying the Queen and the royal party.

This was certainly the most taxing ceremonial broadcast – for both content and scope – that I had ever undertaken, and I was very much aware that amongst the other commentators I was up against the great Richard Dimbleby, who was the master of these occasions. I boarded *Patricia* the day before the event and we had a rehearsal of all the technical arrangements. After this I spent as much time as possible in my cabin, trying to get into my head the various details that might make good embroidery in my broadcast. It was like swotting for a very important exam and I was becoming very nervous and tense. In the event, although I remained tense throughout, the broadcast went smoothly, and the official Listener Research report said nice things, so I must have disguised my nerves adequately.

However, that is looking ahead. I spent the morning skulking in my cabin and getting more and more apprehensive about whether I was equal to the job I had given myself. I began to feel mentally – if not physically – very queasy and was just trying to summon up my courage to leave the cabin, to go over the top at zero hour, so to speak, when there was a knock on the door and Captain Curteis came in. I'll never forget his words to me, which he uttered very apologetically. 'I'm awfully sorry, Robertson' he said, 'I'm afraid the Old Man's up there. There was nothing I could do about it. I hope you don't mind.'

Mind! My mind boggled! The Old Man was Winston Churchill, the Prime Minister, the saviour of civilisation in its worst hour and one of the most formidable figures of history. 'Not at all,' I quavered, or something like that, and followed Captain Curteis. As we came to the bottom of the companionway leading to the aft poop-deck, I looked up and there at the top, in familiar 'They shall not pass' attitude, wearing a naval cap and blue reefer jacket, his cigar clenched above his ferociously jutting jaw was the 'Old Man'.

When I was two or three steps below him he glowered at me and opened fire with 'Who're you?' 'Ppplease Sir, I'm from the BBC.' 'What're you doing here?' 'We're going to broadcast the Fleet Review, Sir.' 'Hmm! Going to menshun me?' 'We'd very much like to say you're present, Sir.' 'Umm! Shpose that's all right – if you menshun the others too.'

That was the extent of my conversation (if you can call it that) with this great figure, but I almost felt that I had been through a severe interrogation by the Gestapo. And this before starting on a broadcast I was frankly terrified of! Nor was it going to be made any easier by the horrible knowledge that a 'Certain Naval Person' would be in earshot. The poop-deck had rapidly become the lion's den.

The Prime Minister was up there because he was one of the Trinity House Brethren, as the honorary members were called. With him was his son-in-law Captain Christopher Soames, who was then his PA. Just before the Review started and while I was waiting to begin our programme, there was a flurry of signals from the royal destroyer and soon a smart Petty Officer of Signals came up on deck, saluted and handed Captain Soames a signal. I hoped that this did not mean that there had been a hitch or that there were any changes in plans which would necessitate last minute re-organising. So I listened anxiously when Captain Soames opened the signal and read it to the Prime Minister:

Signal from the Duke of Gloucester in *Duchess* reads: 'To the Prime Minister. Why aren't you wearing your frock-coat, the same as I am?'

Taking his cigar from his mouth and with a gleam in his eye, Churchill growled:

Make to the Duke: '*Anno Domini* – and purchase tax!'

11

FREELANCE AT A VENTURE

ALL THIS TIME I WAS STILL OF COURSE CONTINUING TO COVER SPORT, AND ALMOST IMMEDIATELY AFTER THE QUEEN'S ACCESSION, before indeed I had time to brood over Peter Dimmock's displeasure, I was wafted away to Oslo for the Winter Olympics. These were not nearly so memorable to me as those first enchanted ones in St Moritz. For one thing the sun didn't shine very much and the atmosphere was greyer. Of the two things I remember most the first was the scintillating success of Jeanette Altweg in winning the figure skating. She was not a brilliantly imaginative free-skater, as had been the Canadian winner in St Moritz, Barbara Ann Scott, but she was a consummate technician, her compulsory figures being immaculately performed. After these she had a good lead but could she hold it in the free-skating against several rivals with more exciting programmes? She did and the whole of Britain was delighted, for she was an extremely modest girl and, having achieved her Olympic Gold, she retired from skating and went to work with handicapped children in Switzerland.

The other memory for me is of repeating my St Moritz effort by doing commentary going down the bob-run. This time, though, it was for television and we had to do it twice. My partner in this venture was Cyril Page, the film cameraman who had been assigned to do the Games. Our allies were one of the American bob-sleigh crews, though only two of them took part – the essential driver and brakeman. Cyril was at number two, immediately behind the driver. Since he had to use both hands to control the camera positioned on his shoulder, it was my job to make sure he

96

remained on the bob. I was immediately behind him at number three position and so was able to put my legs round him and squeeze tight, while at the same time I held onto him with one hand and with the other clung to the bob for dear life.

Fortunately for our safety, we had to go at slow speed or the judder of the bob would have been too much for any sort of picture clarity. We got down in one piece all right and then it was my turn to go again, this time with a Norwegian Storno backpack transmitter and a microphone strapped to my chest. The second run was at full speed and I managed to do a reasonable commentary, which on this occasion – because of the much better transmission and recording quality – was quite clear. The results were sent back to London where they were married together and made an attractive and quite dramatic contribution to the Games coverage.

Ceremonials and Olympic Games were the caviar of rapportage but the everyday life of a commentator/interviewer took me into many smaller situations. One day I was asked to go down to Queens Club for Children's Television and take part in a tennis programme with Dan Maskell. The idea was that the programme would start with Dan serving to me and we would then come to the net and he would start demonstrating various coaching points. On the first rehearsal Dan served to me in the lefthand court, since it suited the cameras better. He put his serve down the centre to my forehand at a speed to which I was totally unaccustomed, but my instinctive reaction made me meet the ball fairly and squarely and my forehand return of serve flashed past him as he came to the net! Naturally when it came to transmission it was a different story.

On another occasion I did a programme for Children's Television with the Lambeth Fire Brigade. A feature of this was to have me going up with a fireman to the top of the long extension ladder to reach one of the highest points in the practice tower. At ground level, before starting, I was helped to do up my safety belt in the correct fashion. Then up we shot. Once at the top I turned round and, looking down to the camera miles below me, said blithely and complacently 'And so you see how safe I am. If a flame spurts out of the window as I am about to climb in and I instinctively recoil, just look, I'm securely belted.' This said, and fortunately before leaning back to demonstrate how safe I was, I glanced down – and to my horror found my belt undone!

Another time Wynford was the victim of the jinx. It was in a celebratory introductory radio programme on the occasion of the opening of the Festival of Britain in 1951. The older generation will remember a peculiarly shaped cigar-like vertical object that seemed to have no visible support (or purpose) and which reared up to a great height – called the skylon. The top of this was to be Wynford's vantage point for one of his graphic scenic descriptions. He performed this well and then started to try to come down but, whatever the mechanism, it had stuck. Although I had been acting as Wynford's number two – from ground level I hasten to say – and felt great sympathy for him in his predicament, I had to leave him to it, because I was due for another broadcast in the Festival Hall.

In the meantime, I was doing more and more television, and by 1953 the number of requests from television to sound OB's, on whose establishment I was, for my services kept increasing, till it got to the point where Charles Max-Muller, my immediate boss, had to call a halt and ration some of his permissions. Much as I enjoyed working for sound OB's, the pull of television was considerable and I suppose it was the realisation that my opportunities for this were likely to be more and more stifled that made me decide to turn freelance and send in my resignation with effect from the end of the year. It was a big step, for I had a family and it would mean living entirely on my wits and experience. Perhaps if I had realised then how cold the outside world could be when once the cosy BBC umbrella was no longer over me, I might not have had the courage to take the plunge. But it seemed to me the opportunity was there and the timing was right, for clearly I was in early on an expanding market, but if I hesitated and remained on the staff I might well lose that lead. So the die was cast.

When I turned freelance at the beginning of 1954 I was determined to do the job properly and decided that I must have an office (this was at home) with a secretary and suitable office furniture. I had no idea what choosing a secretary could be like. A friend offered to lend Liza and me a town office for interviewing. I put an advertisement in the personal column of *The Times*, saying something like, 'Freelance broadcaster needs full-time secretary'. To my astonishment I had shoals of replies and decided I must deal with them as fairly as possible. We sorted out some sixty or so possibles and offered them interviews at my friend's office over two days. It was a terrible experience. Every girl seemed to be the right one for some reasons and the wrong one for others. At the end of the first day we were exhausted. By the end of the second we had not the faintest idea. Then one girl wrote in rather apologetically and late, saying she hoped the job had not been taken. We saw her at home and gave it to her!

Then there was the matter of furniture. I needed filing cabinets and a bookcase. In my enthusiasm and inexperience I bought from an auction room – after some hesitation – three of the largest bookcases I have ever seen. They were beautifully made of walnut in Victorian Gothic style. I paid eleven pounds for them. This was *not* a bargain, because they were so vast and so heavy that nobody, but *nobody* in their right minds would have bought them – at least not in those days. Now they would probably fetch a fortune.

It was three weeks before I dared tell Liza – or my mother-in-law, who lived with us – what I had done. I needn't have worried. When I finally *had* to bring them home they proved too large to be manoeuvred into my house. This was probably just as well, as the women were grim and muttering darkly about 'over dead bodies'.

At the time I was working, among other things, on television's *Panorama*, and I told the sad story to Alfred Wurmser, who used to improvise the programme's special effects. He suggested that I offer to sell the bookcases to Bill King, the television property master. Bill wouldn't buy them, but he did offer to house them for me. So he did, and oddly enough fairly soon – although he had refused to buy them – he started *hiring* them instead. In his own words 'they covered a nice lot of wall'.

Soon they were ubiquitous, and during the next few weeks I was to see them over and over again, passing from one set to another at Lime Grove. They were always accompanied by sweating, cursing, exhausted, scene-shifters who obviously loathed the very sight of them. They began to get very battered.

I rang up Bill to expostulate. 'What!' exclaimed Bill. 'Getting damaged, are they? Well, send in an insurance claim.' However, by this time my eleven pound purchase had earned me some fifty pounds. I felt there was no point in claiming on insurance and having them repaired, only to have it happen again. While I was deciding what to do about it I got a phone call from Bill's boss. 'These bookcases of yours, Max. They seem to be costing us rather a lot. I think maybe it's about time we bought them. Let me see, you paid eleven pounds, I believe.' 'I did,' I said, 'but they've now become rather valuable assets'. In the end we settled at one hundred pounds.

Since that day I have collected many antiques. Some of them have gained in value, others have been bad buys, but the bookcases were in a class of their own. And through Bill King's promptings they started me on a road that was to lead to a whole new area of interest.

It happened like this – Bill and I had become quite friendly, and a year or two later, possibly seeing in me a useful adjunct to his props sources, he suggested I should start buying Victorian type antiques. He had in mind items such as stuffed birds inside glass cases, which would make good dressing for television sets. I took to the idea enthusiastically. So when Liza and I were on holiday in Aldeburgh I used this splendid excuse to satisfy my innate craving for old things, but as yet I did not really know what to buy. So I whizzed round the antique shops, taking a relatively pliant Liza with me, but soon she preferred to stay in the car and read a book – or not come at all. We also went to auctions and at one of these made the acquaintance of a tall chap with an artistic looking beard, who kept dodging about behind us, trying to conceal that he was bidding. Afterwards over a drink he, Charles Morse, suggested that I should meet his partner, Evelyn Butler, who had a shop in the Portobello Road. She was there throughout the week; he only came on Saturdays for the market.

Evelyn turned out to be a delightful, handsome woman whose first interest was Chinese porcelain, especially blue and white. Perhaps seeing in me a prospective customer, she did her best to start teaching me. 'Can't you see the differences between the early eighteenth century and the nineteenth – in the way they painted, in the colour of the blue, in the glaze, in the way the footrim is formed? Just look,' she coaxed. Under her guidance I looked and I pondered and I really tried, but I could see no difference. I thought she was putting on a dealer's act and I despaired of ever learning anything.

One day, however, after giving a lecture in Newcastle, I had a couple of hours to spare, so went into the antique shops on the way back to the station. In the window of one I saw a blue and white bowl. There was undoubtedly something familiar about it. It really did look as if it could be Kang Hsi (the period Evelyn suggested I should collect), for the decoration was alternate panels of flowers and tall, slim ladies. So I went in and after a naive and totally unsuccessful attempt at bargaining I bought it for four pounds ten shillings. Then I took it back tremblingly to London and my mentor. 'It lacks its cover,' said Evelyn – slightly unnecessarily I thought. 'But these long Lizas [the slim ladies] are typical of the period. It is certainly Kang Hsi.'

I had done it! How clever of me! I was hooked. I've collected Chinese porcelain ever since, especially blue and white. In retrospect it seems as unlikely a thing for me to have done as to have earned my living by my voice. The bowl is still one of my most cherished possessions – and it still lacks a cover.

12

PANORAMA

AS IT TRANSPIRED MY DECISION TO TURN FREELANCE AT THE END OF
1953 COULD NOT HAVE BEEN BETTER TIMED. TELEVISON UNDER
Cecil McGivern had decided on what was then a bold experiment –
Panorama. The original conception was that of Andrew Miller
Jones, who had film experience. He visualised 'a topical magazine,
embracing a "wide prospect" of subjects, which would be treated
with respect, humour, humanity or critical investigation as their
sense or the occasion demanded'.

Panorama was not to be *Third Programme* but it was hoped
there would be depth and integrity to satisfy viewers who liked
more than a silhouette.

After *Picture Page* it was televison's first real attempt at a
magazine programme and it had a disastrous start in November
1953, only weeks before I officially became a freelance. The Fleet
Street journalist brought in to front it did not have a chance. Not
only was he new to television, but he was trying to present, or
introduce, as it was called in those days, a programme that had
never been on the air before. Anyone watching that first hideous
display might have laughed or wept because not a single thing
seemed to go right. It was chaos. As a result he withdrew and
Panorama was searching desperately for someone else.

I was an obvious choice in one way, having by now had a good
deal of experience in individual programmes and with sporting
OB's, but was I too connected with sport? Was I competent and
knowledgeable enough to present a programme with a wide
spectrum of the arts and world affairs? The answer was un-

doubtedly no, if anybody had really thought about it. But desperate measures were needed and I was just becoming free, so I was hired.

To begin with I was not only linking but also taking part in many of the items and it was soon clear to the critics, and presumably also to the programme planners, that I was too lightweight for much of it.

Phrases like 'He interviews without fuss and with quiet competence' were the sort of damnings with faint praise that I was apt to get from the critics. However, undeniably my OB experience and ability to think quickly on my feet in live and often fraught situations was helping to pull the programme together and make it a coherent whole. Viewers and critics began to be split between the pro-Max faction and the anti-Max. The latter were pleased when Malcolm Muggeridge, who had conducted some of the items, particularly those with any controversy in them, was brought in to chair the programme while I was engaged with Wimbledon.

The television critic of the *Birmingham Mail* came out with the following:

> I have a grievance to air against Wimbledon. The tennis, I mean. There was not only too much of it on Television yesterday, but it took that nice young man, Max Robertson, away from *Panorama*. That I feel, was a bad thing. The *Panorama* programme has developed into something grown-up and intelligent [sic!] under Mr Robertson. He has become so much a part of it that it was like hearing bad news about an old friend when the announcer told us last night that commentating duties at Wimbledon prevented his being with us. . . .

However, there were those who rightly thought that 'Muggs' was much more the man for the job, if it was to be a controversial programme, and for a while the argument raged. It was eventually a British compromise that settled the issue. I quote from Kenneth Bailey, TV critic of the *People*, when the programme had been running for nearly a year and had finished its first series:

> Remember *Panorama*, the frankest discussion feature T.V. has bred, with its hypnotic dentist, its rabbits with myxomatosis? Max Robertson seemed established as its compere. Then, one night, a Mr Malcolm Muggeridge took his place. Against the quiet and restrained Max the Muggeridge was like a sharp-shooter. He seemed able to demolish any argument put up by

any expert on anything. He voiced doubts, even, about Billy Graham, though he admitted admiring his sincerity. The electric Muggeridge became known as 'Muggs'. The viewers started a correspondence war with the B.B.C. Half of them shouted 'Take him away, leave us with Max!' Half cried 'More of Muggeridge!'

The *Daily Dispatch* even described us as 'Prince Charming' and the 'Demon King'. This was really unfair to both of us, and oddly enough, I found Malcolm, for all his biting wit, to be the essence of charm. The fact that he was editor of *Punch* at the time no doubt accounted for the expansive notices the programme got from Bernard Hollowood and the number of times *Panorama* featured in its cartoons.

As the first series had staggered along until gradually the programme had found its feet and was rapidly becoming something to which viewers were getting addicted, the technical hitches and misadventures of these live performances were legion. Some we laughed at, some left us in despair. I'll never forget the occasion when Jessie, a performing elephant, was due to take part. Her act was to walk on her hind feet and play cymbals with her front ones. It was arranged that she should be brought up in the scenery lift just before she was due to make her entrance. Unfortunately either somebody cued her rather earlier than she should have been or, like any prima donna, she was determined to make a grand entrance and steal the show. Whatever the reason, while we were still on the previous item the lift doors opened and Jessie almost galloped onto the stage, her trunk aloft and the cymbals clashing.

Another time, in the second series, it had been arranged that a Mrs Ada Austin who had been writing bitter letters to the papers about laundries, should air her grievances to a member of the Laundry Association. A publicity photo was taken in rehearsal showing these two contestants shaking hands, watched over by me as referee. On transmission there was no quarter from Mrs Austin. A veritable tirade on laundries issued from her lips as she waved various articles of clothing around and the wretched representative of the laundries, whose name was Payne, began to look distraught. He could scarcely insert a word and it was not long before I was getting urgent signals from the studio manager to bring the proceedings to an end. Not a chance! Mrs Austin was unstoppable – and the viewers loved it. I was even reprimanded by critics for attempting to intervene. This was really the first time that a good row had erupted on television, and it turned out to be such a success that it was the forerunner of many, and eventually led to 'Muggs' taking over that spot.

Meanwhile, I was blissfully presenting a variety of television programmes whilst paying very little heed to the question of dress. When performing in front of the camera in outside broadcasts, there never seemed any particular reason to wear anything but casual clothes – probably usually a sports jacket and flannel trousers. Otherwise in the early days grey was the most acceptable compromise colour for TV cameras. And I had a grey flannel suit, which I probably did overdo. At least I earned the comment once from Ted Tinling (he could fell the most insensitive with one blow) when I appeared in the lunchroom at Queens, 'Ahr, here's Max again in his BBC grey'. Without thought I had taken my outside broadcast attitude into the studio, where again my 'gear' seemed acceptable when performing in sports programmes. *Panorama*, however, was different.

One day the head of presentation, Clive Rawes, a suave and always impeccably dressed man, took me on one side and told me politely but firmly that I really must improve my image. The last time I had had a suit made for me was in 1937 in Sydney, when it had cost thirteen guineas. I still had it and could still wear it! But it was lightweight and in any case perhaps *some* variety was needed. Someone recommended Hawes & Curtis – not the most expensive but definitely good, I was told. So I duly had them build me a double-breasted suit. Yes, suits were built in those days. For one thing the material was commonly much heavier, for central heating was still an exception. I have that suit even now, more than thirty years later, and it can still stand up almost straight on its own.

The programme, although it had fairly regular ingredients covering theatre, books, and the other arts, was also a brantub from which any surprise could be pulled. One such surprise was the oldest person to appear on televison at that time, Mrs Stringer, aged ninety-nine. She had the night of her life and it was a delight to interview her.

Another surprise was a news scoop for *Panorama*, which I was able to provide when wearing my Wimbledon hat, with 'Muggs' occupying my chair. This was the announcement of the engagement on Wednesday 29 June 1955 between the dashing Australian star, Lew Hoad and the fine lefthanded Australian player, Jennifer

Staley. As a star item, we were already using an interview I had filmed with Maureen Connolly about her new role as a commentator for BBC television for, as a result of her tragic riding accident the summer before, as reigning champion, she was unable to defend her title. But even this was eclipsed when I produced Lew and Jenny in the studio and they announced their engagement to the *Panorama* audience.

Lew, as all tennis lovers know, was one of the greatest champions of all time, winning the Wimbledon title in 1956 and 1957, before turning pro and joining Jack Kramer's circus, where he was at once pitted against the great Gonzales. In later years Pancho told me that he respected Hoad more than any other player. Sadly for Lew, his back gave him a lot of trouble and eventually forced his retirement from active competition. He and Jenny set up their well-known tennis ranch in Southern Spain where they still are. He made a comeback for the trial professional tournament in 1967 and again in the first Open in 1968. There were many glimpses of his flair and power, but he had been out of serious play for too long to sustain his effort to a title.

Another item I remember, on a much more serious note, showed us the effects of myxomatosis on rabbits. It was horrific and for those days quite revolting and the protests from viewers were legion. Another story I was concerned with was 'horror comics' and their easy availability to children. Mrs Whitehouse hadn't started up then – and would have found them almost Sunday school reading by today's standards. The more serious side of *Panorama* also dealt – rather too tritely many critics thought – with vast subjects like the hydrogen bomb.

All this time the TV audience was growing very fast and every new viewer was at first fascinated by it. Consequently I only had to appear in public to be almost instantly recognised. I found this extremely embarrassing, although years later when I ceased appearing, human nature of course missed the idolatory! I have always thought that notoriety gained by televison is absolutely false. In those days people only had to appear on the box – without any experience or apprenticeship – to become instant celebrities, while an actor of brilliance, who had spent years learning his craft, might not be able to get stage work anywhere. This worship of TV performers went to such ridiculous extremes that a story made the rounds concerning a Devonshire devotee of Richard Dimbleby's who had actually kissed the hem of his garment.

Andrew Miller Jones had, perhaps unwisely, taken a year's sabbatical at the end of the first series of *Panorama* to do a university course. The editor for the second series was Michael Barsley, who had come from the Features department in radio. Michael had a good journalistic flair but he suffered from a terrible incapacity to make up his mind. Rather like the organisation of Wimbledon, which begins for the next year immediately one Championships is ended, the preparation for a new *Panorama* started as soon as the last was over. There would be perhaps a day's pause for chores, such as answering mail and dealing with newspaper correspondents who wanted to know why this or that in the last edition. Then it was time to start roughing out a few ideas.

The easier ones to begin with were those concerning the arts, for new plays, exhibitions, programmes of various kinds all had their starting dates advertised in advance. However, topicality, even though it was not a news programme, had always been of the essence for *Panorama*. Michael's nose would start twitching about some subject that might only be a small cloud on the horizon but which he felt could well grow. So that would be chased up, contacts made, a view taken. Meanwhile another subject crashed into the day's news with a loud chord, but would its resonances and dissonances last? Still, it had better be looked at. So another hare was set coursing. Just as the first idea was fading as a main topic, the second indeed loomed even larger and it began to look as if he was onto an inspired winner.

So it would go on – idea chasing idea – until the day before the programme when everybody would start chivvying Michael for the script. Alfred Wurmser needed to know what effects would be necessary; 'props' wanted to know what they would be called on for; the designer was beginning to tear his hair on the question of new sets; John Furness, the director, had to get his thoughts and the camera moves in outline; there were many other people with fingers in the pie – not least the secretaries who had to make sure that all those taking part knew what was required of them, and also see that the script was typed, run off on the duplicator and distributed to all concerned.

One very interested party was the presenter, for I had to try to get into my head the order of the programme, the links and bits of commentary that I would have to do live (and therefore memorise), the items that I would be conducting, with the background information on the participants and the line of my questioning. The troops would start converging on Michael's office and battle would commence. Michael hated yielding up his precious running order until the last possible moment for, as sure as he did, a vital news story would break and he would naturally want to include it. Not only would this mean a lot of re-jigging but possibly the rejection of a previously booked item – with its performers, who would not be best pleased. As I eventually seized his 'scrap of paper' from Michael's reluctant grasp and hastened home with it to do my prep, I would have a horrible feeling of insecurity that I might be peopling my mind with stars who would not be shining on the morrow, when everything could well be topsy-turvy. It was perhaps for these reasons that my own particular live outside broadcast experience gave me some real value to the programme.

Meanwhile a new and very powerful influence was being brought to bear on *Panorama* – that of Grace Wyndham-Goldie. She had been slightly junior to Andrew Miller-Jones in the Talks hierarchy under Leonard Miall but, with him away, her woman's weapons and sharp mind had won the day with the Director of Television who was now Cecil McGivern. Power was becoming more and more vested in her, so that before long I coined a phrase, 'Not much could be done or preferment won, except by the Grace of Goldie'.

Grace was now at the helm of *Panorama* and (if you'll excuse the mixed metaphor) as a new broom, she swept with vigour. In the autumn of 1955 she changed the whole structure of the programme. Michael Barsley found fresh television 'woods and pastures new', while Max was given the sop of an interview spot, which was nearly always filmed on some outside subject. Richard Dimbleby was to be the anchor man and many saw this as lending the programme a greater substance. The new editor was also a Michael – Peacock, who never seemed to have any difficulty in making up his mind.

Grace was a most gifted and ambitious woman but at the same time a sort of mother hen of the television scene. She had no children of her own and liked to discover bright young things. Her first protégés of note were Michael Peacock, now given charge of *Panorama* and Donald Baverstock who started *Highlight* and was to succeed it with *Tonight*. They were both graduates of the London School of Economics, both highly intelligent and confident young turks. They had the ball at their feet with little opposition to tackle them.

Another of Grace Wyndham-Goldie's young finds was a certain David Attenborough, who appeared early on in the new *Panorama*, bringing some of his friends from the zoo with him. His naturalness and easy charm won viewers' hearts immediately and it's quite possible that that one *Panorama* item was the springboard from which his huge later success came.

Unfortunately for me I had already been 'discovered' and could in no way be likened to a chick for Mother Hen. Nor had I the new liberal searching anarchic mind that would appeal to her. I think she had a slight sense of guilt for deposing me from my chairmanship of *Panorama*. In the end most people had come to feel I was fulfilling this pretty well after very difficult days of teething. However, that was the old *Panorama* which had been much more of a magazine programme. The new *Panorama* was to be more 'significant', a favourite word with Grace. It would deal with important topics of the day and I am sure she saw it as a mixture of *The Times* and *Guardian* – a heavyweight 'thunderer', which of course in latter years it has certainly been.

Round about this time Grace reluctantly agreed to try me as an interviewer on *Highlight*. When I arrived for rehearsal I found myself in the hands of a young trainee producer called Alasdair Milne. His instructions to me were very firm. He gave me three questions to ask and said I must not, on pain of death, depart from them or supplement them in any way. He had evidently been warned that I was an ad libber by nature, with no great intellect.

The man I had to interview was Roy Brooks, an estate agent who had made a reputation for himself by his extraordinary methods of promotion. These methods consisted of running properties down so amusingly that people became intrigued. For instance, he would run an advertisement something like this: 'A half derelict, rat-infested, sub-basement flat – admittedly with a discreet garden and understanding neighbours – might be let to any unsuitable tenant.' These are my words, but they are the sort of thing he did, and he had made a name for himself by it.

The interview started and I asked the first question. I needn't have bothered. Roy Brooks simply used it as a launching pad for a long monologue extolling Key Flats – for which he was the agent. And I, with all my professional hairs raised but cowed by Alasdair's strictures, let him do it.

After the programme there was *uproar*. And the next morning the press had a field day – the BBC advertising! There were shock waves across the nation. And there was of course an enquiry. Both Alasdair and I had a lot to answer for to the Head of Talks, Leonard Miall, normally a most benign person. It seemed I had thoroughly blotted my copybook this time, and I didn't get another chance with the programme. And, as everyone knows, Alasdair Milne went on to become director-general.

In almost suicidal despair, my spirits were raised by the prospect of a non-BBC job that I was offered out of the blue. Apparently my chairmanship of *Panorama*, and the fact that I was appearing in a variety of television programmes, had decided the organisers of the British Film Industry luncheon for comedians that I was the man to host the occasion. It was held at the beginning of August 1955 at the National Film Theatre on the South Bank Festival site. The leading comedians present were Tony Hancock, Terry Thomas, Benny Hill, and Richard Hearne (Mr. Pastry). I never was quite clear what was expected of me, unless it was to spark off a brilliant exchange of wit between these famous entertainers. What I had forgotten – and most people do – was that most funny men are very serious and only comic when they have a good script, written by professional joke-makers. My memory of the occasion was of it being very heavy going and the only sparks that seemed to fly were those of professional jealousy. Depression returned and in the end I felt as lugubrious as Tony Hancock habitually looked.

In my quest for new fields to conquer, I was involved in another television débâcle in the summer of 1959. This had nothing to do with Grace or *Panorama*, but was – or should have been – a pleasant little interlude. I had been summoned by BBC's Midland Region to help show the flag in a big way in East Anglia, since commerical television was about to start up there. They conceived a twenty-five minute programme called 'East Anglian Special', to be centred on Oulton Broad, and cast me in the role of presenter, feeling, I imagine, that I was thoroughly reliable and they needed a sure bet.

The programme was planned to start with me in a Norfolk brown boat, a special sort of sailing boat, talking to its owner, Ted Chamberlin, a broadcaster himself. I was then to interview locals on a variety of themes particular to the district. There would also be music in the shape of an accordionist and towards the end of the programme a brass band contingent from a nearby American Air Station. Finally, after an interview on crop-spraying, I was to be whisked away in a helicopter whilst the credit captions rolled. It was a well-balanced programme.

Those were still pretty primitive days and we had no intercom between me in the brown boat and Malcolm Freegard, the producer, in his OB van. It was arranged that on the wave of a handkerchief by the SM on the jetty, I would welcome viewers and proceed to interview Ted Chamberlin on the intricacies of brown boat sailing while he brought us smoothly into the jetty when I would step ashore to continue the programme.

I had worked with Malcolm before and should have remembered that he had a similar capacity to mine – of attacting the unprovoked and unexpected. During rehearsal we established the right distance from the jetty for us to start the programme, so that the two-and-a-half-minute interview I was to do with Ted would bring us nicely to the landing point. What nobody had allowed for was that the convenient breeze we had had during rehearsal would suddenly die completely. The handkerchief was duly waved and I made everyone welcome. I then turned to Ted and interviewed him. Suddenly I was aware that we were not moving – or at any rate barely creeping towards the jetty.

The interview was getting longer, the time for the rest of the programme shorter. Unfortunately, the next item was another interview. There was no two-way communication. I had two transmitter microphones (one as back-up in case of failure), with their batteries, one in each trouser pocket. I had to get ashore. I was fast becoming desperate as agonisingly Ted inched her in. It was time for heroic measures.

Stepping up onto the gunwale with brave abandon I said to Ted, as the gap slowly narrowed to about seven or eight feet, 'I think I can do it, don't you Ted?' and with that I leaped. Well, I hadn't allowed for one or two things. Firstly, that the world record for a standing jump was eleven feet. Secondly, that I was standing at about a foot to eighteen inches *below* the level of the quay. The next thing I was aware of was being up to my thighs in water, with my arms wrapped around a bollard, peering over the top of the jetty at a craned camera some forty yards away.

Quite unable in the circumstances to carry on with the interview that was next due, and *with complete aplomb* I went into a hastily reconstructed cue to another item. By the time the helicopter removed me from the scene of this disaster I was a shivering wreck. What this episode did to the ratings battle between the BBC and ITV, I have no idea.

111

Coming back to *Panorama*, for my interview topics, which were invariably filmed, I was lucky, to begin with, to be working most times with Dick Cawston and occasionally later on with Tony de Lotbiniere, a cousin of the great Lobby's. Some of my outstanding memories of these assignments were interviews done at the Tower of London, when some recalcitrant jackdaws refused to caw and had to be coaxed rather in the Steve Wade manner by somebody sliding along the ground out of shot with tempting morsels. The birds still refused, evidently feeling that somebody was trying to poison them.

Once we visited a transport cafe near Grantham in the small hours and by concealing the camera at the start I got some really off-the-cuff views from lorry drivers. These were an eye-opener for many viewers, making them aware of the long hours and difficult driving conditions that these men often had to work under. The dangers of falling asleep at the wheel were vividly and frighteningly described by one man.

We also did a story on coffee bars and I particularly remember one we visited in the King's Road, which was the gathering point for many youngsters. With the help of the proprietor, the camera and the microphone were again concealed, though the extra lighting would have given the game away to anyone suspicious. I was able to get some very real and heartrending confessions of the aimlessness and boredom of some of these boys and girls. Again many viewers were seeing a side of life that they were totally unfamiliar with. The hidden camera technique was also used to entertaining effect in recording the inane remarks that we are all of us capable of making when watching others at work – in this instance men digging a large hole for building foundations.

One *Panorama* story that gave us a lot of fun in the filming was about rag and bone men. They were natural talkers and comics – and philosophers at that. When that compelling series *Steptoe and Son* later achieved the same sort of popularity as *Yes, Prime Minister* today, I could not help feeling that possibly the brilliant scriptwriters, Messrs Simpson and Galton, had got their original inspiration from seeing our *Panorama* item.

We even had Roland Emett and his famous steam engine, Effie, on the programme. I can't remember what set of lines we took for our *Panorama* journey but I don't think I ever enjoyed a programme more. Playing deadpan stooge to Emett, I asked the sort of leading questions that enabled him to discourse learnedly as

Professor Emett on these creations of his imagination. Apparently many a viewer believed the whole conversation to be deadly serious, if somewhat confusing. I treasure a copy of Emett's *Home Rails Preferred* with an illustration by him of 'Effie' specially drawn for me in the frontispiece. He signed it with the following inscription, 'For Max, to mark the first appearance of Effie in England, on the occasion of her backing into *Panorama*'.

My most exciting assignment for the programme, however, was covering an archaeological dig in the City of London. It was a rush job against time in the foundations of what was about to be one of the soaring new buildings that make up the modern City of London skyline. In those foundations the site of an ancient Roman temple of the god Mithras had been discovered. The London Museum was in charge of the dig which was proceeding as fast as scientific care allowed, for there was a building deadline to be met. I was sent down with a camera team and arrived at the actual moment that a marble head of the god had just been prised from the clay it was embedded in. I was allowed to help splash water over it, clean off the muck and then hold it tenderly. It was the most wonderful experience – almost a feeling of live contact with our ancestors of two thousand years ago.

Once we went to Rome, whence Mithras had been imported – this time to do the whole programme from there. I had the usual sort of stories allotted to Max – interviews with children at an international school; a look at Ostia, Rome's dormitory seaside resort; and an interview with Prince Massimo and his wife, the actress Dawn Adams. Trust Richard Dimbleby to be given the plum job – interviewing Sophia Loren. I was lucky to be allowed to be present and have drinks afterwards, since the interview was held in a most romantic setting on a flat castellated roof of an ancient building overlooking the glorious panorama of the Eternal City. Magnificent though the vista was, most of us were more concerned with the beauty at hand.

Looking back over the years, it is interesting to note how much *Panorama* changed. It is also extraordinarily rewarding to have been in virtually at the beginning, and to have had a hand in its successful launching.

13

SPORTING OCCASIONS

O N THE RE-START OF TELEVISION AFTER THE WAR, SPORT COULD AT FIRST ONLY BE COVERED ON FILM OR IN THE STUDIO. OBVIOUSLY Television Newsreel included many sporting items but it was not until outside broadcast units started to become available that sport was covered in the field. Some of the early programmes dealt not necessarily with the most important sports but often with minor ones, whose administrators were only too anxious to propagate their sport; whereas those at the helm of the already popular ones tended to look askance at television, in case it kept spectators away from their grounds. Apart from this the minor sports were very often more flexible and easier to demonstrate.

Obviously major events were also dealt with as they occurred, but another reason for sticking to smaller ones was that to cover say Wembley or Lord's meant a much larger deployment of cameras – still in short supply. In the summer of 1950 a little cohesion was brought to bear under the monthly title *Television Sports Club*, which in the new year changed to *Television Sports Magazine*. To the best of my memory, this was always conducted as an OB in some large hall – for instance, on the 24 January 1951 it was in the London Scottish drill hall. The mix was a variety of sports demonstrated in technique and interview and all performed – by sportsmen and production team alike – in rather an amateurish fashion, for the inherent skills and polish were still in the process of evolving. Programme-making as yet lacked a depth of tradition and the patina that comes with it.

Paul Fox, who had started his career scriptwriting for television

Newsreel, realised that there was a real need for a regular studio programme on sport, and by May 1954 he had achieved his object under the now famous title *Sportsview*, of which he became editor. In the first *Sportsview* I interviewed that superb tennis player and lovely person, Doris Hart and also Britain's longjumper, Sheila Lerwill. Afterwards I brought them home for dinner with Liza and me.

Paul Fox's number two was Ronnie Noble, a cameraman of vast experience in every field, having covered the Korean war and many news items of all kinds including sport. These two formed a marvellous team. Their energy was boundless. So were their persuasive powers. Anything they set their sights on – whether an individual or a sporting body – was subjected to a barrage of promises, cajolings, threats (covert or open) until they achieved their end. They were real 'operators', made for television, and they earned the title of 'the Mafia'. It was not long before they could also have been called 'the Professionals', for that is exactly what they were. Anyone working for them soon became professional too – or no longer worked for them. Despite the mailed fist, they were an extremely likable pair – both being born leaders – especially Paul. Working for them, as I often did as an interviewer and commentator, and occasionally, as front man (regularly for a while for *Junior Sportsview*), life was always invigorating.

I first met Ronnie when I was covering the 1952 Summer Olympics in Helsinki for our overseas services. He was on a roving commission with his news camera and we saw quite a lot of one another. So it was that together we found ourselves involved in the marathon on the final Sunday. The strong favourite for this was Britain's Jim Peters, but there was a dark horse in the field, Emil Zatopek of Czechoslovakia who, despite this being only his first marathon, could never be written off after his amazing distance performances in the 5,000 and 10,000 metres in London – and again in Helsinki where he won both titles. By the halfway stage Jim was leading, with Zatopek in attendance. We were told afterwards that he was actually talking to Peters (possibly good gamesmanship) and asked as any innocent tyro might, 'Are we going fast enough?'

The press following the event were being transported in a large bus just ahead of the leaders. Ronnie and I had taken up our positions on its roof, so that he could get some good shots of the runners and I could do a little bit of commentary on my portable recorder. Suddenly, at just about the three-quarter mark and when the bus had momentarily stopped, Jim Peters fell out by the side of the road, clearly in considerable distress.

Ronnie and I were off the bus in a flash. He was shooting from the hip and I, having for once remembered to start my recorder, went straight in, thrusting the microphone in front of Jim's face. I'll never forget his despairing expression as he simply said. 'I'm sorry, England. It's me darned legs!'

The really disappointing story from a British point of view was the failure of Roger Bannister, who was the strong favourite for the 1500 metres. To me he seemed to have that look of self-doubt on his face as the cameras concentrated on him at the start. In a close finish he was never really in it, coming fourth, the race being won by in an electrifying last ten-yard burst by the Irishman Delaney. In the 5000 metres, for which he was strongly fancied, Chris Chataway was lying very handy on the final bend but half stepped on the kerb and stumbled. So Britain's two great runners failed to finish in the medals.

As well as being a great privilege, covering an Olympic Games is also a marathon for the lucky commentators selected. There is all the preparatory work in watching as many events as possible (in the commentary field allotted to you) leading up to the Games themselves. As ever the commentator is like the examinee approaching the fatal day. He is trying to take in and retain as much information as possible, so that when the appropriate moment arrives the background to any performance can be naturally sketched in, providing depth and form to the picture being painted. During the Olympics the work was very hard but exciting and stimulating. The hours were long but one kept going as long as need be. At the end of it all, exhaustion took over.

The 1956 Olympic Games were very widely separated, both in time and distance. The first were the Winter Games which were held at Cortina d'Ampezzo in the Italian Alps in January/February. The Summer Games were in Melbourne and did not take place until the following December. For me the Winter Games had been a race between the birth of our second child and my going out to Cortina. The baby was due in mid-January but nothing happened . . . and nothing happened . . . until it got to the point that I had to obey the old creed of 'the show must go on'.

For Cortina it was again a compact BBC team that was reporting. Peter Dimmock was fronting the programmes for

116

television, also doing some interviews and a little commentary.
Ronnie Noble was the editor and director of our TV efforts,
working with our Italian hosts in the studio. I was doing radio
reports for all services, as well as being frequently used for
television. It was not quite St Moritz again – for one thing it lacked
the Cresta – but very nearly. The exhilaration of working hard and
knowing that much of one's work was getting on the air was there.
Peter and Ronnie were enjoying themselves – especially when they
got a rise out of me. This was very easy since, as I have said before,
I'm fair game for anyone with a straight face! Ronnie, particularly,
was always the instigator of a bit of buffoonery and ribbing. His
attitude did a lot for our morale when the going was tough and
tiring.

My main memory is of the final Saturday, the last night of the
Games. I had a very difficult assignment on my hands – the ice-
hockey final between Russia and the U.S.A. Ice-hockey is a
difficult sport to commentate on. The pace is very fast and the
change from attack to defence instantaneous. This also makes it
very difficult for the cameras, and player recognition is paramount.

Waiting tensely for the beginning of the transmission, with the
usual starting-gate nerves, I heard the announcer in London cue
over to me with the words, 'And now for a commentary on the
final of the ice-hockey match between Russia and the U.S.A., we
join our commentator in Cortina, Max Robertson. . . By the way,
Max, congratulations on the birth of your son!'

My mouth was already open to pour forth a commentary.
Completely taken aback, I managed to stammer out something
like, 'Thank you very much – but now for the ice-hockey final.'
Knocked off my perch, as I was, it took me a little while to get
going.

The match over (it resulted in a win for Russia by 4 goals to 3), I
rushed down from my commentary position, which was somewhere in the overhanging beams of the roof, to get to our
temporary studio in the bowels of the stadium. I knew that I had
little time, since the ice-hockey commentary had led straight into
the final overall programme looking at the Games in retrospect. I
got into the studio with a minute or so to spare and settled myself
down beside our leading woman skier, Addie Pryor. She had
suffered the misfortune of breaking her leg which was now encased
in plaster. I knew I had only one and a half minutes for my interview
with her and again was very much on the *qui vive*, for it only needs a

slight false start and the balance of such a short interview is ruined.

Peter Dimmock was in the chair and in his smoothest manner cued over to me, 'And now we join Max Robertson, who is talking to Addie Pryor. By the way Max – 8 lbs.' Again I was just ready to go in the Addie Pryor direction and again I was pulled up. 'Thank you very much,' I said, totally inadequately and – now thoroughly disconcerted – stumbled lamely through my interview. Apparently my confusion was very much enjoyed, not only internally but by the public. In retrospect I had the consolation of knowing that this was only the third announcement of a birth on television, the first two being those of Prince Charles and Princess Anne!

On the following Monday I flew home. Changing planes in Paris, I bought a *Continental Daily Mail*, and retired to mind my own personal business in comfort. Turning to the back page, as was my wont, I was aware of something vaguely familiar and suddenly realised I was staring at a picture of Liza in bed holding our son. The caption was 'Introducing Marcus'. So that was how I learned his name – under the circumstances an appropriate ending.

I think a slight digression is allowable here to relate another of perfidious Peter's bons mots. One day in the autumn of 1957 I was booked by *Sportsview* to interview Floyd Paterson, not a natural for me, since boxing was not one of the sports I normally covered. However, I enjoyed interviewing and during the programme, while waiting our turn, was doing my best to get my homework right and put Floyd at his ease.

I was keeping my eye on a monitor, but only half listening to what Peter Dimmock was saying, as he introduced another item, when I suddenly became aware that he was dramatically keeling over at his desk, murmuring as he did so, 'Max, I can't go on, you take over'. Trust Max the Reliable. It was a crisis and I leaped in to cover for him, somehow managing to both link and interview until Peter appeared to be recovered enough to wind up the Programme. Afterwards I went home, feeling that I had done a good job and saved both Peter's face and *Sportsview*'s.

Next morning I felt even better when a national newspaper carried a dramatic account, headlined, 'PETER HID HIS ORDEAL FROM VIEWERS'. It continued, 'There was drama behind the TV cameras last night, a drama in the show-must-go-on tradition, which viewers may have guessed at, but did not see. For the BBC cameras were switched away from a flu-weakened Peter

Dimmock a split second before he collapsed over his desk. . . Max Robertson was able to take up the talk smoothly.'

It was a long time after I discovered – I think Peter himself told me in an indiscreet moment – that far from feeling ill, he had suffered that unnerving experience of the teleprompter breaking down in mid-stream. He had not been a war-time pilot for nothing – his avoiding action being immediate and brilliant. Max carried the can, rather like a dog wagging one on his tail.

To my chagrin – but no great surprise – when the BBC team to cover the Melbourne Olympics was announced, my name was not on it. I was the only commentator who had been to every Olympics since the war, but I knew that I was being left out for economy reasons, since I was now a freelance. Also, the boss of sound OB's was going this time, which cut the 'effectives' down by one. The fare to Australia and all other expenses involved had obviously been taken into consideration. Nettled, I wrote to my old boss in the Australian Broadcasting Commission, Huck Finlay, who was now the deputy general manager, asking whether I could be considered as part of their team, since I knew they were starting their television service on the springboard of Olympic Games coverage. The answer was enthusiastic and I felt that I could cock a quiet freelance snook at the administrators.

It became a family affair when Liza managed to get an assignment to work for *Woman's Hour* and *Illustrated* and BOAC very kindly helped us with our passages. I was one of the ABC team covering both the athletics and swimming. In the first the outstanding memory was of that very determined athlete, Chris Brasher, winning his Gold medal in the steeplechase. As he and the Norwegian, Ernst Larsen came over the penultimate hurdle together it did rather look as if Brasher's flailing elbow might have thrown his opponent off balance. Larsen staggered and lost a lot of ground. Chris got home by a narrow margin, from the fast-closing Hungarian, Sandor Rozfnoi, with Larsen third. Nowadays this sort of thing happens all the time but then it was regarded as 'interference' and therefore punishable by disqualification.

There was an immediate protest, as a result of which Brasher was at first disqualified but later, after an enquiry, he was re-instated. Pending the outcome of the enquiry, all the British press, who had hungered for a medal and something big to write about, besieged the room in which Chris was barrackaded. Among them was Paul Fox, who had managed to come out mainly, I believe, for the

Overseas Service. Liza, with whom Chris Brasher got on well, managed to reach the door, purely for the friendly purpose of telling Chris how sorry she felt for him in the circumstances. The door was opened a crack and, just as Liza was about to go in, she felt a sharp kick on her ankle and muscleman Paul Fox was through, whereupon the door was firmly closed. Paul got the scoop interview he wanted.

My main memory of the swimming was of the delightful Judy Grinham gaining her Gold medal as expected in the backstroke, with her great home rival Margaret Edwards third. Judy could always be relied upon to give a happy interivew and I was as delighted for her as much as for Britain.

My work had now finished but next morning Liza was due to interview the members of Ceylon's hockey team, who had done rather well. It was arranged that she should go out to do this in the Olympic Village where Brian Brake, the photographer working with her for *Illustrated*, would meet her. So I drove her out in the Landrover, which Rovers had very kindly lent us, both for ease of transport in Melbourne and so that we should be able to do a film trip for Children's Television immediately after the Games. It was quite early for a Sunday morning and the streets were pretty deserted. Melbourne was built on a grid system and soon we took a left turn onto the main route to the village. Determined not to be late, I was tootling along at a fair pace and became vaguely aware that there was a slow-moving procession of cars ahead of us. From a distance it looked like a funeral and, being in a hurry, I felt no disrespect would be shown if I went past. I had only passed two vehicles when I suddenly realised it was not a funeral at all but a royal procession, for in a blinding flash I remembered the Duke was paying an official visit to the British team.

I was in a predicament, for I realised that there were probably special passes for the day which we didn't have, so I did the only thing possible in the situation. I pulled in ahead of the last two cars. Fortunately a Landrover has a sort of semi armoured-car look about it and could well have been an official vehicle taking up station a little late. No motor-cycle policemen came to investigate us, as undoubtedly they would have done in these terrorist days, and we proceeded sedately. I began to feel that with luck we would get in – if a little late.

To begin with it was rather fun and Liza even began to gesture her hand regally towards the cheering crowds that were now beginning to line the route. That was all very well but, as the crowds grew denser and denser and the cheering increased in volume, my neck began to turn very red under my collar and I had serious misgivings that we might soon be arrested – for *lèse majesté* at least. As the head of the procession reached the Village, so it started to concertina and our Landrover, which we had nicknamed Gladys (from GLY, the letters of her number-plate) soon, in our fevered imaginations, began to stick out like a sore thumb. The cars inched forward as they passed through the main gate.

Just before we reached there the anguished and incredulous face of Brian Brake appeared at my window. There was a very quick and fiery exchange. First he wanted to know what on earth we were doing and then, saying, 'You need an extra pass and I haven't got one,' he demanded to be taken in. I felt our position was precarious enough and growing more dangerous by the moment. If we were seen attempting to smuggle someone else in, we could *all* end up in clink! I let the clutch in and left behind an apoplectic Brian, who I observed in my mirror gesticulating murderously. How we got through the gate I don't know but, as the procession started to move on towards the British quarters, I took a hasty right turn and sped away from what at any second was going to be acutely embarrassing.

Liza got her interviews. As to how Brian Brake fared, I'm not too sure. I think he did manage to talk his way in, as any good photographer would, but I knew I would never be forgiven for my dastardly desertion of him.

Let me digress for a moment from the Olympic Games to the 1958 Empire Games in Cardiff. So far I had been covering athletics and swimming pretty regularly for television, whenever they occurred as individual events. At Cardiff I was in the team for both, which was asking a lot, for the swimming began before the athletics finished. Later I was to discover that Paul Fox had often been viewing the athletics in the company of David Coleman who, from the comfort of an armchair, was able to point out the odd mistake. As a result – and because David was a miler of at least County standard – Paul made up his mind that, come the next Olympic Games in Rome, David should commentate on the athletics, while I stuck to swimming.

Actually, though my pride was hurt by this at the time, it was a good decision. Not only was David more versed in athletics but, with television becoming increasingly more professional every day, it was really impossible for one man to concern himself with both sports. He would be quite unable to spend all the preliminary time necessary to get to know the performers of the world properly as they trained.

For the swimming I was paired, as the BBC professional race-reader, with Harry Walker, who had been an international water polo player and in the administration of swimming for many years. I knew nothing about swimming and can confess now that I loathe it! However, so long as I was only concerned with race-reading, I felt I could do a reasonable job. Harry, in his enthusiastic Brummigam voice, was the filler-in of aquatic knowledge and technical know-how. We became quite a 'Mutt and Jeff' act. I was to cover swimming with him until I finally lost my contract with television outside broadcasts at the end of 1970.

Of the postwar Olympiads, Summer and Winter, I covered every one until my last at Mexico City in 1968 – with the exception of the 1960 Winter Games, which were held in Squaw Valley, California. With a probable dearth of medals to report and winter sports still not widely enough followed by the public, the expense was thought to be unjustified. However, the Summer Games in Rome more than made up for missing them. Not for nothing has Rome been called the Eternal City. It is the most magic mixture of old and new.

Although *Sportsview* was by now a regular midweek evening touchstone for all sports lovers and *Grandstand* was into its stride embracing the big Saturday events, this was the first time that the BBC had mounted such a large operation to cover the Olympic Games on television. Paul Fox was in charge and at his best. He had a true journalist's flair for the big story, a very quick and certain mind for making operational decisions and the ability to inspire good work from his team. I was doing the swimming with Harry Walker and found myself fully engaged by that.

I have two main memories of thse Games, the first being Anita Lonsbrough winning her Gold medal in the breaststroke and the tremendous boost to everybody's morale that her success stimulated. But I was furious when the interview with her was given to David Coleman to do. He had already deprived me of doing athletics and this seemed to be adding insult to injury! I think Paul realised my feelings and, out of a sense of fairness, when that great Australian runner, Herb Elliott, won his fifteen hundred metres

Gold medal, I was given that interview to do – much, I believe, to David's chagrin.

The swimming events having ended, I was free to watch Herb Elliott's race, for which he was the undoubted favourite. His coach, Percy Cerutti, was known to have chosen a seat at a good strategic point, where Herb could pick him out during the race and read his semaphored instructions. These were delivered by Percy taking off his shirt and waving it, though what the code was only Herb knew. Percy was certainly observed to wave it and the result justified his doing so, for Herb accelerated at the right point, moving smoothly away from the Frenchman, Michel Jazy, and won majestically in the new Olympic record time of 3'35.6

It had been agreed that when Herb could break away from press interviews he would come over to where we had a television camera set up in the BBC area. It was my job to shadow him and make sure he did. So I managed to get down to the subterranean room where he was changing. While he was doing so, he was being questioned by Terry O'Connor of the *Daily Mail* and I quietly sat by, making a mental note of any good questions. Terry threw me one or two curious looks which I blandly ignored. When he had finished and Herb was ready we went over to the BBC enclosure for the interview. I found Herb fascinating to talk to – or rather to encourage to talk. He was a considerable thinker about his sport and about life in general. He gave me a cracking interview and Paul was very pleased. I had felt slightly badly about Terry, for I knew that there was no way that his interview could be printed and read before television had scooped him.

My next Olympic sally was to the Winter Games at Innsbruck in 1964. By now, owing to the far greater coverage allowed, I was restricted to the downhill skiing events and the ski-jumping. Though I was sorry not to be following one of my favourites, the bobsleigh, I had quite enough on my hands. My highlight memory was of doing commentary on the second run of the men's slalom.

The times of both runs are added together to give the competitor's total, the lowest deciding the winner. We were nearing the end of the second run, with Austria's Josef Stiegler, one of the first-round leaders coming down. He flashed through the finishing gate and the clock on my television monitor stopped. Don't forget that in those days the computer had not arrived. There was no immediate total shown, no instant adjustment of the relative positions of the leading runners. My mental arithmetic, usually

123

fairly reliable, told me that Stiegler who had just finished had won the gold medal by fourteen hundredths of a second.

Despite being utterly concentrated, I had known for some while that standing behind me, listening and watching, was Bryan Cowgill who was in charge of production. He was a redheaded Mancunian with a fairly short fuse, and his presence didn't help, for when doing a commentary of this kind, involving such quick mental adjustments, one does not want one's mind to be clouded by the boss's shadow.

Realising that Stiegler had a good chance of taking the title, I had been working my description up to a peak of excitement and, as the clock stopped, I yelled something like, 'He's got the Gold!' Imagine my consternation when Cowgill, at his loudest and most forceful, screamed behind me, 'You've given the wrong bloody winner!' I was aghast. My confidence completely evaporated. I was in fact proved to be right, but Bryan stumped off without a word of apology.

At the Summer Games in Tokyo, Harry and I were again doing the swimming. As television commentary became more and more specialised, I was increasingly aware of my lack of knowledge in swimming technique. I tried to compensate by learning more and more about the swimmers as individuals, so that I could provide human interest to bring them alive. As a result I spent my entire time at the pool and saw nothing of Tokyo – except for one Sunday visit to see wonderful examples of their porcelain and pottery in an International Exhibition they were holding to honour the Olympics.

In the swimming events Britain's main hope was Bobby McGregor in the 100 metres freestyle. In the World standings for the year he was only just behind the best American swimmer Don Schollander. It was a tremendous race. Bobby turned first and was leading all the way down the last length. I have never been so excited in a swimming commentary and was giving it my all. With about five metres to go, and Schollander smoothly accelerating, I knew instinctively that Bobby might be on the wrong arm and lose the touch. As I was screaming agonisedly 'He's on the wrong arm', that was exactly what happened and I have seldom felt so frustrated – for Bobby, for Britain and for viewers. It was just like looking at the training film again of the 1932 1500 metres when I had so badly wanted Jack Cornes to win. Schollander's time was 53.4 seconds – a new Olympic record.

In 1968 Grenoble was the scene of the Winter Games and of the fantastic performance of a son of France, Jean-Claude Killy, who won all three downhill skiing events. He had just won the Downhill and I was relaxing after a demanding commentary, when I was instructed – rather peremptorily I thought – by Jonathan Martin, one of Bryan Cowgill's lieutenants, to 'get Killy' for an interview. 'Go and get him yourself,' I thought but, ever the paranoid freelance and thinking that perhaps after all it was my duty, I burrowed into the maelstrom around Killy. Eventually, despite official attempts to bar me, I actually managed to prise him loose and started to bring him to Jonathan. I didn't get far. I rather think I must have been stealing him from French television. Whatever it was, they didn't like it and I was promptly arrested. Broadcasting in France was never without its hazards!

My last Olympic venture was at Mexico – again with swimming. The main difficulty at this venue was in acclimatisation – both to the height and the change in time zones. The latter proved to be the more difficult and I never really expunged the previous day's tiredness by a decent night's sleep. At the stadium our working area was several floors below the 'dubbing' suite, where commentary was added to edited film. There was either no lift for this bit, or it was always too crowded, so it meant a trudge up the stairs for about three floors – nothing to a fit person at ground level. At 6000 feet it was exhausting and one had to climb very slowly and allow several minutes to get one's breath back before trying to do a commentary. Bearing this in mind brings the strain on the athletes into vivid perspective.

In the pool the most memorable moment – certainly for our hosts the Mexicans – was the final of the breaststroke when their star swimmer Felipe Munoz, with his high-bobbing style, was surging down the last length well in the lead. In all my life I have never heard such pandemonium, as the crowd chanted in rhythmic unison 'Mun . . .yoth . . . Mun . . .yoth'. A chord of my memory told me that troops always had to break step crossing a bridge, in case the synchronised vibrations of a standard march brought it down. The effect seemed to be just the same now, and I almost felt a sense of physical fear that the roof would cave in. It was a relief when he finished, for the cheering then became continuous.

The incredible achievement was the winning of nine Gold medals by that remarkable American swimmer, Mark Spitz – a record that has never been bettered, nor is ever likely to be surpassed. But the

125

overpowering – if distasteful – memory was of the American sprinters who, standing in victory on the rostrum, used it as a political platform and gave the clenched fist Black Power salute. It seemed a total denial of the Olympic concept and an insult to its founder, Pierre de Coubertin.

In 1965 the World Bobsleigh Championships were held in St Moritz. It was seventeen years since I had been there, in that enchanted world of the 1948 Olympiad. For once Britain had strong contestants, particularly in the two-man boblets. They were Tony Nash and Robin Dixon. In a very exciting contest, which we covered on television, they duly won and Britain had the unusual experience of celebrating a Winter sports Gold medal.

When the four-man bobsleigh competition was being held, in which Britain gained no medal, I began to feel again the necessity to go down the bob-run once more. I was in my fiftieth year and I felt I had something to prove – if only to myself. Robin Dixon, who sensitively divined my feelings, very kindly gave up his seat on a practice run. Alan Smith of the *Telegraph* euphemistically reported him 'unwell' as a cover-up for me being unofficially included. The other crew members were Tony Nash – driver, Guy Renwick – number two, and Robin Widdows – brake. We went down at full speed and I don't think I have ever been so scared in my life. It was all I could do to cling on, and the sense of relief at the finish almost superseded the exhilaration of the run. 'Never again!'

After the Winter Olympic Games at St Moritz and Oslo there was no consistent coverage of winter sports on television until the start of Eurovision which, to the best of my memory, kicked off with ski-jumping on New Year's Day 1957 at Garmisch-Partenkirchen. This became an annual event for me, until New Year's Day 1971, which was my last sporting broadcast for television.

I had been the BBC's first winter sports commentator, and for years – since coverage was comparatively small – I was the automatic choice to report everything from bobsleighing to ice-hockey. I remember once, in the early days, being sent to cover the World Skating Championships at Garmisch. I had no experience of skating, and axels, double axels, and the various other spins and jumps were performed too quickly for my untrained eye to recognise them. (Looking back, it is extraordinary how versatile we were expected to be.) Luck was on my side, however, for the British champion, Michael Booker was not taking part and helped me out as race-reader. He knew each skater's programme so well that he was able to say, 'double axel' or whatever the evolution was, in good time for me to say knowledgeably, 'And now for the double axel'. Alas, Michael departed to Canada and I was without my prop next time. It wasn't very long before Alan Weeks took over!

I now realise how fortunate I was. In these days of specialisation no one has the variety or the opportunities which were mine. Of course it was *exhausting* – and nerve-wracking. But looking back, well, it was a lovely time, and I wouldn't have missed it for anything.

14

COMMONWEALTH VISION – A CHILDREN'S CRUSADE

A MAN IS SUPPOSED TO BE AT THE PEAK OF HIS POWERS AT ROUGHLY FORTY. IN 1956 I WAS FORTY. EVERYTHING WAS GOING VERY WELL. I was still doing *Panorama* (if only as a roving reporter); I was constantly being used in outside broadcasts of all kinds; and it was my best year in club cricket with the BBC.

I suppose I was at my most confident when one day my imagination started me thinking about Britain and the Commonwealth – and why it was that, as one of the major powers, who had been victorious in two world wars, we were now so weakened in our will, our material assets and, most important of all, our influence in the world. Even then there was talk of the Commonwealth being finished as a force that mattered. As a family of nations it was also in real danger of suicidal behaviour that would lead to its break-up. I felt that this impending disintegration was due in part to ignorance and racial predjudice.

It was with these thoughts in mind and a vague plan outline that I approached the new chairman of BOAC, Sir Miles Thomas, with a view to enlisting his aid. What I had in mind was that BOAC could possibly make an aircraft available – to be called perhaps 'Commonwealth Vision' – and that a film unit could then fly to all parts of the Commonwealth, shooting, editing and producing films rapidly on the spot. My idea was that by showing people to each other a greater understanding would result. However, although Sir Miles was interested, he felt the time was not right for him to act. Eventually, after putting out a couple of other unsuccessful feelers, I decided to do what I could in a small way myself. I approached Owen Reid, head of Children's Television, with the suggestion that after the Olympic Games in Melbourne Liza and I should make some films, along the above lines, especially for children.

He lent his support enthusiastically to the idea – with the proviso that he could not fund the operation in any way, but would merely give me air time for a series if the material was good enough. It was a challenge and we accepted it.

Rover's had already lent me a Landrover and, during the Games I had become friendly with Stanley Hawes, the head of the Australian film service. He kindly released for our use a sound camera and one of his cameramen allotted to the Games for a week after they ended.

The cameraman's name was Frank Bagnall and he probably didn't relish the idea of a week more away from home. His attitude from the start, which he made no effort to conceal, was 'How on earth did I get myself mixed up with these Pommy amateurs?' He was right, of course. Although I had been in front of a camera fairly often, I had never directed and had no real idea of the technique.

Our object was to drive as far inland into the 'outback' as we could on our way to Sydney. This meant a sort of Great Circle Bearing, our track being an arc between Melbourne and Sydney. The idea was to film anything or anyone we saw that might be of interest to children back home. The first two nights we spent at Tatura Sheep Station, being splendidly entertained by Jim Trevaskis and his family, and getting reasonable material including kangaroos on the hop. On the third day we went on driving through flat, brown, bare countryside – with never an object of interest to film. Frank was getting more and more bloody minded and I was quite despairing. We knew that we were approaching our nearest point of real 'outback', from which we would have to retreat towards Sydney.

Daylight was fading as we came to a few ramshackle-looking houses, in front of the largest of which we lit upon a magical scene. Grouped on the edge of the verandah were four children and a pony. Between them they had a huge ice-cream cone, which everybody – including the pony – was in turn having a lick at. Even Frank was galvanised into action. In a flash we were all out of Gladys and feverishly setting up camera and recording – to the huge amazement of the ice-cream guzzlers. We just got them as the sun disappeared, and that short sequence proved to be a high point of our 'Six Days to Sydney', as the film series was eventually called.

This little place was called Morundah which, the children told us, had a population of 130, thirty-two of them children. Next morning in the bright sunlight it certainly looked like a last outpost, but when we enquired whether we were really in the 'outback', the children replied with disbelief, 'Naow, the "outback's" over there,' waving vaguely towards the far shimmering distance. Morundah was an Aboriginal name with two meanings. The nice one I have forgotten but the libellous one – in the dry state we observed, anyway – was 'stuck in the mud'.

Perhaps it was more fitting metaphorically, for to the children we must have appeared like visitors from outer space. We had a wonderful time interviewing them about their pets, toys and pastimes. They seemed so spellbound that one of them clearly forgot a family duty. Suddenly his father, a lean rather sinister looking man, walked purposefully straight into our little group and, without any acknowledgment of our existence, removed his son by the ear. Clearly he felt that our's was a foreign and evil influence.

We filmed Morundah's star turn – an emu the children had befriended as a youngster and named George. But in growing up George underwent a sex change and laid an egg. She was hastily re-christened Georgina and ruled the main street in no uncertain terms. It was wise to keep a wary eye on her, for she had a lethal kick and needed little excuse to use it. She gave us a very jaundiced look when the children presented us with her egg – already blown, I hasten to say.

The rest of the trip was less memorable, though it at least took us to Gundagai, where there is the famous Australian statue of 'The Dog on the Tucker Box'. Banjo Paterson immortalised in verse this legend of the faithful friend who kept vigil on the only belongings of his dead master, a prospector. Another fabulously named place that we had to go through was 'Wagga Wagga'. From there our route led us through Canberra, where we got something in the nature of a scoop when Liza interviewed the Prime Minister's wife, Dame Patti Menzies. We reached Sydney by our six day's deadline, enabling a slightly softened Frank Bagnall to report on time for proper duty. We still had one or two chores to do, mainly recording wild tracks of the sounds of Gladys starting, changing gear, accelerating and stopping, to cover any awkward gaps in our filmed sound.

When the films were finally shown on Children's Television some months later, we were able to cover any unprofessional continuity gaps by live commentary in the studio, mingled with shots of us doing our linking narration. It was all very amateurish but quite new for those days. Indeed, we were the first on British television to do a series of this kind with sound – involving people. David Attenborough, following Armand and Michela Denis, had already started his famous nature films, but he had the advantage of dealing with animals, whose various growls, grunts and shrieks could easily be synchronised with pictures.

We had brought home various trophies or small examples of curious things we had seen, useful objects to be used as props in the studio. One was Georgina's egg, so that naturally gave rise to the title 'The Emu's Egg' for our first programme. The second, mostly concerning our visit to Tatura Sheep Station, was 'Kangaroo Hop'. The third had as an ingredient pictures of us helping to put out a baby 'bush fire'. It seemed harmless at the time but such fires need only a little fanning to endanger homes and livestock.

The fourth programme was called 'Dog on a Tucker Box' in memory of the statue at Gundagai. In the fifth we visited Koala Park in Sydney and the highlight of the programme showed these delightful little creatures, second perhaps only to the giant panda in heartwarming popularity with all ages of Man; so what more natural as a title than 'Up a Gum Tree'. The last programme 'Sail Ho' was all about the little VJ sailing boats that almost every Australian child seemed to have. They were incredibly safe and manoeuvrable. No wonder that Australians grow up completely at home with surfing and the sea.

The series proved to be popular with children. Indeed, the name Morundah could no longer be translated as 'Stuck in the Mud'. It had become the most famous place in Australia, and scores of letters reached it from children in Britain – all asking for pen-pals. We received an agonised entreaty from the schoolmaster of this little place saying they could not cope and he had had to write to an Australian national paper asking for recruits to help out Morundah's children in replying to the British. In a small way we had really hit the jackpot.

I was so encouraged by all this – and so was Owen Reid – that we decided to try again, on a more ambitious scale if possible. Our first

131

idea was Kenya and the High Commissioner was very keen that we should go there. However, it proved to be too difficult, owing to other commitments I had at the best season for the job. Finally, I decided on the West Indies, which were still under the Colonial Office.

We had got away with just having one cameraman in Australia. But Children's Television could not afford to send one with us and I realised that I would have to take a chance. Someone put me onto a chap who they said was a very good amateur cameraman, Ion Trant. We met and he seemed to like the idea, so we decided to go ahead. The trip was going to involve five to six weeks in the early spring of 1958, and I was determined to visit as many of the islands in that time as possible.

Making arrangements for a trip of this kind called for considerable organisation and goodwill. Whatever I lacked in the first was made up by the second, for everybody involved proved to be extremely helpful. We were doing this at a good moment, for it had not been attempted before and the islands were still unsophisticated enough to welcome the publicity they hoped they would gain.

It was a fantastic trip and never – even at an Olympic Games – have I worked so consistently hard for so long. Not only was I having to drive myself, but I was being a slave-driver to Liza and Ion. At times relations became strained and there was mutiny in the camp. However, in the end we did get a lot of material that was of interest to children and, indeed, to adults as well.

Liza and Ion covered Barbados, since I could not get away in time for it. We then in turn visited Trinidad, British Guiana, Trinidad again, Grenada, St Vincent and the tiny island, Becqui. It was at the last that we came upon the most extraordinary scene as we came over the crest of the island's one big hill. On the track leading down to the beach, on which the island's industry, boat-building, was performed, we came across a local politician (the population was in the hundreds) doing his canvassing from a very old jeep. His enthusiasm was boundless and his catchphrase was, 'I want you to come out in your voting numbers to support me'. This he repeated *ad nauseam* – even when his sole audience appeared to be a rather sardonic looking goat.

We had a week in British Guiana – all too little to try to get in the variety of interesting subjects. We were fortunate to have as a guide in Georgetown MacDonald Bailey, the great sprinter who had won the AAA sprint titles for so many years running, and whom I had interviewed when covering athletics. He was the local information officer which made our job so much easier. It was through him that I got an interview with Forbes Burnham, the Leader of the Opposition, who was later to be Prime Minister. What he made of our strange little unit, I don't really know, but what politician will turn down the chance of a platform?

Liza always recounts the story of how, when I was busy arranging another venue, she and Ion went off to film an anaconda that two locals had caught. While they were shooting a sequence the anaconda suddenly freed itself and made straight for our intrepid pair. Ion, with his head buried, was slow to realise that the superb shot he had was becoming a larger close-up at every second. Yelling, 'You're not insured for this!' Liza pushed him to one side – just as the anaconda shot between them at speed, making straight for its natural habitat, the river behind them.

The outstanding memory of British Guiana came after we had filmed a story on open-cast bauxite mining and refining. The local PR asked if we would like a flight in their company seaplane to the top of the Kaieteur Falls. We grabbed the chance. The sight as we flew over the lip of the falls was breathtaking. The vast volume of water plunged over and dropped 740 feet to rebound in gigantic spumes of spray. It was all the more awe-inspiring because the river, until it emerged at the lip of the fall, was almost invisible in the jungle-covered plateau. As we looked back we could see the enormous spreading bush-covered plain stretching away for more than a hundred miles.

We came skimming in over the lip and landed expertly on the comparatively narrow river half a mile up from the falls. Ashore there were a few huts and several grinning Amerindian children to welcome us. This tiny settlement contained the official Government rainfall station. The man in charge had grizzled white hair and an engaging smile. I interviewed him on his duties, which he said were to measure the rainfall at dusk and dawn. This did not sound unduly arduous, so I asked him 'What do you do when you're not measuring the rainfall?' A broad grin broke out on his face as he said, 'Man, I jes relaxes!'

We did our interviews at the top of the falls. It was very humid so we carried our gear from the landing point in two journeys, leaving Liza alone at the falls when we went back for the second load. Having just recovered from the anaconda incident, it didn't do Liza's confidence much good when one of the locals said, 'Me see alligator on that side, Missus. You no worry him, he no worry you.'

In Grenada our main story was on the growing, harvesting and curing of nutmeg, which was the island's main industry. A fascinating diversion from this was to go and look at a natural phenomenon at one end of the island, where two little coves – separated by the thinnest of isthmuses – were entirely different in appearance. One had normal white sand, the other was completely black. The contrast at such a small distance apart was striking.

In St Vincent they were very proud of the sea-island cotton, which needed careful growing but was so rewarding when produced, for it has exceptionally long and fine silky fibres, from which a very delicate but hardwearing material was made. You don't hear much of it these days, so presumably it has been superseded by man-made fibres, if so alas for the economy of St Vincent which then largely depended on it.

Jamaica was our last port of call. In those days sugar and sugar-cane were very much the staple products – presumably today they have suffered, since medical research has influenced most people to eat far less of it. But Jamaica has gorgeous tropical fruits and bauxite as well. That was mainly exported to Canada to be converted into aluminium, for which there was such a wide demand.

These films finally made eight programmes for Children's Television under the overall title of 'Come to the Caribbean'. Our technique was much the same as for 'Six Days to Sydney' and children enjoyed them very much. We had been trying to carry out my original 'Commonwealth Vision' idea, endeavouring to show our children and their families at home what the life of children and their families in the West Indies was like. Obviously we were only scratching the surface but, judging by the interest aroused in viewers, there was definitely something in my idea – and there was tremendous satisfaction in having carried these through off our own bat.

These two series, which we would never have been able to film under modern union rules, had aroused some opposition even then. As we sent our 'rushes' home for processing, it was very easy for the professionals in the film department to give vent to loud criticisms of our lack of technique and continuity in producing what were contemptuously called 'happy snaps'. What they did not know was that the way things had been planned continuity would be provided live by Liza and myself, talking in the studio.

134

Such complaints did not help. More seriously, word I think was going round that 'Max was trying to do too much'. While I was away I could not take part in sporting programmes. When I tried to suggest another series, Owen Reid supported me but, when the controller of television, Kenneth Adam was approached, I soon became aware that there was opposition abroad. Feeling that Liza and I had proved our point with the two series, I asked him to fund another one. Though he seemed genuinely interested, he did not feel he could. He also dropped a hint that I might well be doing myself no good, for Paul Fox wanted to use me pretty regularly in Sport, and apparently did not take too kindly to my going off for such long periods.

As I have said before, Paul I always found to be a fair man. Knowing that I had paid £2,000 or so for the sound camera that we had used in the West Indies – and perhaps feeling a little guilty if he had intervened with Kenneth Adam – he it was, I think, who probably influenced the film department to hire the camera regularly until most of the capital had been paid off. But – I had lost my 'Commonwealth Vision'.

15

GOING FOR A SONG

IN APRIL 1964, I WAS AS USUAL COMMENTATING ON THE BRITISH HARDCOURT CHAMPIONSHIPS AT BOURNEMOUTH WHEN MY NUMBER two, George Pagan, a member of the engineering staff at Bristol, said casually, 'Max, you're very keen on antiques, I know. Would you be interested in taking part in an antiques programme we've started at Bristol, called *Going For A Song?*' 'You bet I would', I replied enthusiastically. 'In what capacity?' 'Well,' said George, 'They're not very happy with the chairman. The trouble is he doen't know anything about antiques.' I could well understand that being a bar to chairing such a programme successfully. I would have hated to be in such a position. I reiterated my complete willingness and the upshot was that he reported back and I got a telephone call from the producer of *Going For A Song*, John Irving (the grandson of Sir Henry Irving), whose initial idea the programme had been.

John asked me if I would like to come and take part in the programme as one of the 'customers', ie the amateurs, who had first guess at the objects before the experts told us all. This I did a couple of times and could see that this was a programme that was right up my street. The chairman, an Irishman whom I had never heard of before, was perfectly competent but lacked the touch of the initiate and the confidence that went with that. After the first programme Arthur Negus, already established as the resident expert, told me how he had always admired my work and hoped that I would become chairman.

Well, I got the job and felt how lucky I was. Lucky, too, that I was able to cut my teeth while *Going For A Song* was still being transmitted as a regional programme. It began to get such good viewing figures and reactions that the first network series was started that autumn. Its success was undoubted from the very start. With Arthur Negus (whose personality was visibly enlarging with every programme, and his following multiplying fast) as the mainstay – and perhaps because my experience and calm style was giving it shape – it could hardly fail in the antique climate of the time. To the best of my belief this was the first series about antiques (as opposed to antiquarian and archeaological objects) ever produced on British television. Ordinary people were thirsting for the knowledge that they saw the experts expounding without any trickery before their very eyes – and very often there was humour in the mix that made it good entertainment. Many people viewed it for vastly different reasons. A sergeants' mess wrote that they ran a book on the prices.

The programme was lucky, too, in having producers who were interested in the subject. John Irving started it but before very long migrated to North America and the new producer was his old assistant, John King. John had been a jack of many trades and an antique dealer for a while, so he had the enthusiasm, experience and contacts to collect together the people and objects that were needed. Also, in its initial stages it was fortunate to have Lobby's analytical mind, (he was now controller of West Region), which was largely responsible for ironing out any rough edges and finding the right format – simple though that might be.

In fact the format changed very little during the thirteen overall years of the programme's existence. Many will remember it, but perhaps I should give a short description of how it worked. Arthur Negus was the resident expert. Having lived all his life in the environment of antiques, first being brought up on his father's cabinet-making bench, then having been a dealer for some years and finally the cataloguer for the respected Gloucester auctioneers, Bruton Knowles, he had a very wide knowledge. But nobody – as many viewers came to believe of him – can be expert in everything. Arthur's main subject was English furniture, but he also had a good knowledge of silver, English porcelain and glass.

Moreover, Arthur had those most precious of gifts in the antiques trade, a good eye and an astounding memory. He only had to hear a tip from an expert once and he would remember it. In some later programme it would come out quite naturally and this ability largely helped to create the aura of encyclopaedic knowledge with which viewers soon credited him.

In each programme he was partnered by a visiting expert, whose particular field would be where the emphasis of that programme lay. The expert would sit on my right, Arthur on the wing. On my left would be two 'customers', one from either sex, the girl beside me. There would be a succession of objects lined up in the right order to give the visiting expert one in his field first and alternately thereafter. The object, revolving slowly on a turntable, would be seen by the viewers, who would also hear an official description that was denied to those taking part.

When the turntable stopped the object was handed to the 'customers', who each ventured their opinion. Their job was to be intelligent, amusing, glamorous – but ideally not too knowledgeable. A 'customer' who knew too much tended to spoil the show, leaving no leeway for the experts to indulge their connoisseurship. The 'customers' were always the most difficult ingredient to get exactly right. Many of them were stars of stage, screen or television who – if perhaps temporarily 'resting' – would be only too glad of the exposure in a programme of rapidly increasing popularity. Some would find it very difficult to think their thoughts aloud, which is what the viewer loved hearing. Others would give voice to inane thoughts. There was no greater cause for irate letters from viewers than their very often conflicting opinions of the 'customers'.

They having delivered their verdicts, I passed the antique across to one of the experts, depending on whose turn it was. They discoursed learnedly – Arthur always with earthy humour and caressing gesture (particularly if it was applied to a piece of furniture) that viewers adored – and the visitor, sometimes struggling with his own nerves at a first television appearance, with varying degree of humour and expertise.

The piece was then passed back to my desk and I turned to the 'customers' for their 'bids' as to what they thought this piece would reach at auction, while at the same time the experts were writing their valuation down on a piece of paper which they surreptitiously handed to me. It was the average of their two prices that the 'customers' were trying to arrive at. Points were scored by the 'customer' nearer to the experts, and after a while I introduced ten points if they were within ten per cent, five points otherwise. The winner on points received an antique prize to the value of ten pounds. A tradition grew whereby, if it was at all a close thing, I usually contrived by the right hint or two to let the lady win.

At the beginning the winning 'customer' always appeared again, to be challenged by a new one next time. This had led to some considerable embarrassment as the first regional series came to its climax. A girl called Carole Brown proved to be invincible and remained undefeated as the series ended. It was only just in time, for she had been growing visibly more pregnant and her baby was born shortly afterwards. When the programme returned in the autumn on the Network, Carole was one of the first 'customers', but largely because of the experience gained with her, a new rule was instituted that a 'customer' could appear only three times, however success-ful. Carole again was undefeated – winning, if I remember rightly, nine times in all – a most extraordinary record.

It was a mercurial mix of personalities that I had to try to steer and keep in balanced relation for time, subject and good humour. Sometimes it was magical, at others the resulting dish was not quite as appetising as we had fondly anticipated, considering the intrinsic interest of the antique ingredients.

It was this very unpredictability of the quality of any programme that in some ways gave it its spice. The viewer felt an excited expectancy as each piece appeared on the turntable and followed with eager interest as the experts' knowledge unfolded. That was an especial fascination, watching the antique surgeon probing and dissecting.

But things could go wrong. An expert in European porcelain, Michael Newman, acknowledged by all as one of the most knowledgeable in this field, on his first appearance in *Going For A Song*, showed every sign of first-night nerves. To his relief when the first object appeared on the turntable, it was something he knew very well indeed – a fifteenth century Italian maiolica piece made at Gubbio. He expounded on it learnedly and I could see Arthur taking every word into his mental computer for future reference.

When his next specialist piece came up, Michael, full of a nervous performer's euphoria when he knows things are going well, having seen it at a distance on the turntable, knew instantly what it was. When I put it into his hands he didn't even look at it but launched forth into a paean about this marvellous seventeenth century Dutch Delft dish. The only snag was that it was not ten years old, a brilliant copy made in Devon.

I have never been so happy in television as when working with

Going For A Song. It wasn't work, it was sheer pleasure. It was especially exciting while the programme was 'live', or at least, 'live' recorded, meaning that it was recorded straight off without any chance of correction. My early outside broadcast experience of live situations, which could be as uncertain as unexploded bombs, stood me in very good stead. The main difficulty was in timing the programme, which was only twenty-five minutes long, so that we ended without an undue sense of rush or any piece being skimped.

This was not at all easy, for so much depended on the varying talkativeness of the 'customers' and the enthusiasm of the experts. A knowledgeable enthusiast is always good entertainment, so that I felt like a butcher (and was often called one by viewers) when I had to stop somebody in full spate. Arthur was by now a veteran broadcaster and knew just how to take the slightest hint from me, but the same could not always be said for his partner.

People often used to ask me if he was as nice as he came over on television. The answer was undoubtedly 'yes', but there was a slight qualification. He was like an avuncular bear, whose claws were normally sheathed. However, if he thought that anybody was getting at him (he was very sensitive at heart) or needed disciplining in any way, there would be a rapid transformation and the culprit would not know what had hit him. He was a very good friend to me and it was a great honour to be asked to edit his book *Going For A Song – English Furniture*.

As the programme matured and became more and more popular, so it attracted more interest in the papers and more and more people sought to appear on it. It was a wonderful way for actors to remind producers of their existence, and it soon became a battle-ground between the main London auction houses, Sotheby's, Christie's and Phillips. If an expert from one appeared on the programme, he had to be balanced by one from another. It was rather like the balance sheet of party political broadcasts. Individuals, too, realised that if they could show their expertise on the programme, they would be more highly regarded as authors of books in their field, or as dealers to go to for advice in collecting.

Another aspect of the programme was the vying with each other of private owners, collectors and museums to have their pieces shown. Not only were they getting a free valuation but often added knowledge about family heirlooms. Whereas in the beginning it had not always been easy for the producers to find a good mix of objects, there was now an *embarras de richesses*. From time to time

140

John King's policy on the type of objects would change, depending on whether we were getting criticised for being too rarefied and esoteric in what we showed. The argument would be that people wanted to see more everyday articles, specimens of which they might find in their own cupboards. Valid though this appeared at first sight, I'm convinced that most viewers really preferred to see and hear about exceptional and precious antiques that really exercised the minds and skills of the experts.

Arthur, who had started the programme still as the cataloguer of his firm, had brought them so much business and notoriety (the local aristocracy were competing with each other to have Arthur go round their homes) that he was very quickly elevated to a partnership. His prestige was colossal. He had started aged sixty-two and had immediately blossomed, for he had real star quality.

He loved it and the audience loved him. Having realised early on that people enjoyed seeming him caressing furniture with his familiar round-arm gesture, the producer asked him to make sure to do this. One word was enough and thereafter Arthur's sweeping, loving gestures became even more pronounced.

The programme was also bringing me recognition again – some welcome, some not. It was very nice to feel I was involved once more with a successful studio programme, in contrast to the many outside broadcast commentaries I still did. What was maddening was to realise suddenly that I was no longer anonymous when doing my antiquing for my collection. I discovered, especially in the junkier shops (where in the old days a real find could be made), that often I had only to touch something for the dealer concerned to think that it must be good. Sometimes, if I enquired the price, I would get the answer, 'Oh, I'm afraid that's just gone. I'm sorry, I should have taken it out of the window.' Either that, or if a price was given I had the feeling that it had suddenly become magnified.

Although the main structure of *Going For A Song* never altered, at various times John Irving and John King tinkered a little with the internals. 'Arthur's Competition' was the most integral of the programme's side issues. Its position varied from halfway to being the last item. Other ideas that never really got off the ground, for the simple reason that they took up too much mainstream time, were 'Puzzle Piece' (which explains itself), 'Attic Treasure' (viewers were invited to submit pieces that had lingered un-appreciated in their lofts), and 'Saleroom Piece' (an ingredient supplied for a while by Sotheby's and Christie's – something that was coming up soon for sale and that was of particular interest).

'Arthur's Competition' was very popular both with viewers and the production staff. It was a winner all the way, an enticing bait for 'viewer participation'. To begin with the competition usually came somewhere in the body of the programme but, probably to make room there for one of the other short-lived trial items, it was moved to the end. In many ways this was the sensible place for it, but it made my life far more difficult. To arrive at the conclusion of the programme, leaving just the right amount of time for the competition was a high-wire juggling act. The resulting fat mailbag of postcards was very reassuring. On the other hand, silly correspondence which needed an answer, was not only an irritation but a waste of the time of a small and very busy unit. For example:

Dear Sir,

In your last programme you showed a group of a shepherd and shepherdess. It was extremely rare and valuable, being so your expert said, an almost unique example of Chelsea porcelain in its best period. The value your experts put on this was £550. We in our family have an exactly similar figure, which has a large red anchor marked on its base. Can you tell me whether this would make it even more valuable?

Yours faithfully,

P.S. I forgot to mention that one arm is missing and one head has been stuck back. However, I'm sure that in such a rare piece this would make no difference.

Well, it sounded reasonable enough, but damage always affects the value, particularly at periods when the public are not buying antiques eagerly. If it were a very rare piece, the damage would not matter so much, for there would usually be at least two parties (be they collectors or museums) who would compete for it. However, the bull point that the correspondent made, namely that the piece (so like the Chelsea one shown) bore a *large* red anchor mark, was actually a gross blemish on its escutcheon. It was almost certainly a copy – probably by Samson of Paris. Imagine two or three hundred enquiries of this kind at the end of each programme, very many of them not nearly as reasonable at first sight, and you can understand how that particular mailbag was dreaded.

The early years of *Going For A Song* were far more pleasurable from my point of view. Once Ampex recording had come in our recordings would be constantly stopped for some petty little fault – a boom microphone being glimpsed, an unfortunate shadow cast, a camera movement not being perfectly timed, a tiny hesitation or repetition of speech – countless little things. Once this happened seventeen times in the recording of a twenty-five minute programme. Apart from my feelings, the damage done to the confidence and naturalness of the other participants was often irrevocable. Frequently the director, perhaps at the mercy of the technical staff, would sacrifice spontaneity and humour in the search for an artificial perfection, the like of which very often gives a meretricious gloss to today's programmes.

The sort of rough edges that the direction was trying to erase were the very things that brought reality to television. Nowadays, some directors realising this, inject a simulated roughness but it is not the same thing.

Another difficulty I was up against was my natural desire to chip in on oriental pieces, but the producer emphatically disliked me showing any knowledge at all. This always irked me. Indeed, there was one occasion when, if they had taken my opinion on an oriental piece, they might have been saved some embarrassment. It was a Chinese blue and white figure of the sixteenth century. This had come from a dealer, who had dated it sixty years earlier than it should have been, making it out to be approximately 1515. I knew perfectly well that, at the earliest, it was about 1575 and probably a little later. The producer, however, categorically refused to change the official description.

Fortunately, the expert on the day was Anthony du Boulay, head of the oriental department at Christie's. It was all I could do to refrain from 'leading' him. I needn't have worried. His opening words were something to the effect of, 'Ah, a nice example of a Wan Li figure'. The Emperor Wan Li reigned from 1573 to 1619. Innocently, I asked, 'Are you quite sure, Tony, for there is an opinion that it was of the reign of Cheng te [1506–1521]?' 'Of course I'm sure,' said Anthony. 'You know perfectly well, yourself, that it could not be earlier than Wan Li.'

Despite its tremendous popularity, at the end of each series the production staff, Arthur and I always wondered whether there would be another. When it came to the last programme in one series, *Gong For A Song* No 13, which went out on 18 June 1972, we had been definitely told that this would be the end of the road;

and I have now in front of me a nostalgic souvenir, for I got everybody concerned with the programme on that occasion to autograph the front page of my script. Arthur wrote' 'May our friendship, born of this Programme, never wane'. 'Perhaps I'd make a better ball boy!', wrote the losing customer, Virginia Wetherell; whereas the winner, Peter Cushing struck a rather higher note with, 'Max, may God's blessing be with you always . . . in all sincerity.'

But after a three-year gap the programme rose again like the phoenix and endured until the end of May 1977. The last series took place out of the studio in famous houses and, I felt, that in striving to be a bit different, it was losing some of its real tradition. That tradition had varied little over the years. As we've seen various small ingredients had been tried and found wanting. The two that stood the test of time surely owed their long life to the personality of Arthur. One was his competition object, the other his piece of furniture. When *Going For A Song* first started this piece was always the third in the programme and was unknown to Arthur. Let me quote from my foreword in his book:

> Arthur has endeared himself to millions who think of him as the last word on 'antiquity'. . . Not for nothing has he been called 'Willie Woodworm' and to watch him turn a piece of furniture upside down, investigate its antecedents and almost unerringly find any bar sinister on its escutcheon, is at once an education and entertainment.

The public were entranced by his performance, but not everybody in the trade applauded so readily. No man is infallible and sometimes, no doubt, Arthur did make slight mistakes, but jealousy magnified them and Arthur, a sensitive person as I've already said, found the burden getting too much. In future it was agreed that he would choose the piece of furniture and bring it to the programme. It gave him the chance to investigate it properly but, to my mind and I think to most viewers', his performance was never quite so real. Watching his mind at work in a live situation on a piece he had not seen before had a supreme quality as compared with the slight artificiality of glossed rehearsal.

In looking through my old *Going For A Song* running orders, I have been amazed at the famous names that took part. Leslie Crowther loved coming, for he was a real collector of pot-lids and parian ware. Glancing down the list I pick out at random from the men Osbert Lancaster, Graham Hill, Michael Bentine, Bernard Miles, Nicholas Parsons, Ted Dexter, John Arlott, Humphrey Lyttelton, Tim Brooke-Taylor and, going back a bit, that deep chocolate voice that used to say, 'And the next object is. . .' in *Twenty Questions* – Valentine Dyall. Of the women Isobel Barnett, Phyllis Calvert, Fenella Fielding, Moira Lister, Jane Asher, Marjorie Proops, and Antonia Fraser.

After the programme and a quick drink in 'hospitality' most of the cast would be returning to London by train. Since it was not easy always to get food, the programme provided us with what we thought of as *Going For A Song* Doggy Bags – cold collations that were hugely unappetising. But, washed down by British Rail wine and plenty of good conversation and laughter, they sufficed. I always enjoyed those journeys. However, *Going For A Song* had by now survived for a run of thirteen years (including the break). It had provided really good viewing and for me the greatest fun. But at long last the 'Song' was gone.

16

INSIDER OUTSIDE

ALTHOUGH I HAD ALWAYS FOUND THE RÉCLAME OF TELEVISION DIFFICULT TO COPE WITH GRACEFULLY, I HAD NATURALLY enjoyed the 'inside track' that it gave me. I had become spoilt by constantly being recognised and the fuss that went with it. Good service, best seats, no queueing and all the other perks that go with being a 'personality'. With the loss of my television OB contract at the end of 1970, I soon began to notice the difference, though *Going For A Song* compensated to some degree.

It was not so much that I wanted to be noticed and recognised; it was far more the feeling that I was no longer there when sporting history was being made, nor helping in my commentary to reflect the occasion. I think that's the most difficult thing to bear when the TV mantle has gone. Perhaps the biggest disappointment and sense of loss was to know that never again would I be part of an Olympic Games.

Looking back on my behaviour of the time, I feel I reacted much as I did when I was a flying cadet and practising a forced landing approach. As the horrid line of telephone wires loomed into my conscious vision, I had taken what seemed the obvious (but actually stupid and highly dangerous) action of pulling back on the joystick and lifting the nose of the aircraft just over, as she staggered into what could have been a fatal stall. Now I pretended to myself that the loss of my contract, instead of being the start of the slippery slope, was just one of those things. Something else would turn up and until it did, ostrich-like, I tried to bury myself in 'antique' sand. I spent more and more time at the salerooms, finding less and less

146

that I either wanted, or could afford, to buy. It was frustrating and sometimes led to mistakes – buying for the sake of buying, under the cloak of rarity or intriguing shape or design, damaged things; or even worse going into a 'foreign field' and making a beginner's mistake.

With the demise in May 1977 of *Going For A Song*, which was shortly replaced by *The Antiques Roadshow*, for which I, alas, was not called upon, my interest in antiques was now truly purely in collecting. In my field of seventeenth and eighteenth century Chinese porcelain, this was getting more and more prohibitive. The chances of finding an odd piece in travelling around the country were becoming very slender. This was largely due to a much more widespread knowledge amongst general dealers who, even if they did not know exactly the period of a piece, could now usually recognise that it had some quality and value. Perhaps not knowing how much they could charge and, in any case, often not having the right clientele locally, they would themselves take it straight to either Sotheby's or Christie's. In the past many such dealers would have been in awe of the big salerooms and have avoided going to see them. *The Antiques Roadshow* soon put an end to such diffidence. Private people were also encouraged to sell their belongings through the big London salerooms.

Pieces of seventeenth century 'Transitional' porcelain which had been relatively unwanted when I was one of the first to start collecting it, were now 'desirable'. So I found myself attending sales but not being able to buy the things I wanted. It was very frustrating. I tried to get interested in pieces of a later period that were still affordable, but found I simply could not. Yet, it was important to keep going to sales if possible, for otherwise I very quickly lost touch with collecting trends and values. It became even more difficult when in 1978 Liza and I went to live in Alderney.

However, I did have a small antique crusade in 1977. It was Wimbledon's Centenary Year. One of the main projects to mark this occasion was the building and opening of the Wimbledon Museum, most handsomely designed and executed by Robin Wade. With the opening of the museum in mind, when on any of my antiquing rounds, I would vaguely keep an eye open for tennis memorabilia. I was in a junk shop in the Croydon Road, looking as usual for oriental porcelain. Finding none, I was just leaving when some instinct made me turn to the proprietor and ask, 'You haven't anything to do with tennis, by any chance?' Giving me an odd look,

147

as though summing up how much of a fool I might be, he replied, 'Well, there is a portrait of a lady tennis player somewhere, it's not much of a thing.' Finally he found it behind a pile of other pictures. Once unearthed it proved to be an oil of a girl seated at a garden table, a tennis racket over her knee and her hair bound with a bandeau. It was signed Sidney White and dated 1924. There were two large holes in the canvas – fortunately not on the figure. The face was confident and determined looking.

'1924' I mused to myself. That was Biddy Godfree's first title, when she was still Kitty McKane. Could it be her? Yes, I suppose allowing for age it might be. I bought the picture and at the first opportunity rushed to the telephone. 'Biddy,' I asked, 'when you won Wimbledon in 1924 [and beat Helen Wills in the final to do so, the only loss that great American champion ever sustained at Wimbledon], did you have your portrait painted? 'Yes', she said, 'I did.' 'Was the artist's name White?' 'Yes,' it was. 'Why didn't you have it?' 'We couldn't afford it,' she replied. That picture now hangs in the museum during Wimbledon and in Biddy's sitting room for the rest of the year.

Luck was again with me on two other occasions of this kind. I was attending a house sale deep in the country and, in sorting through a stack of dirty old prints and impossible pictures in a vast brass tub, I came across a lovely water colour of a fresh-faced, fair-haired girl in a black ruched dress, standing on a lawn against a background of trees, about to serve underarm to her invisible opponent. It was signed with a monogram on the righthand bottom corner that was either E.R. or E.B.R. In the lefthand corner opposite was the inscription, 'Match-ball, Strafford Lodge, April 25th 1877'. That was a very significant date, being two months before the first Wimbledon Championships and only three and a half years since Major Walter Clopton Wingfield had marketed his garden game under the original title of 'Sphairistike' – later to become 'Lawn Tennis'.

I was not able to stay for the sale and left a bid of about £50 which, to my chagrin, failed. The buyer, I discovered, had paid £90 for the lot. He was a dealer, so I was able to get his address, being determined by now to have that picture. I telephoned him and he still had it. Knowing by my persistent follow-up that I was really keen on it, he was demanding £90 for it alone. I fell.

The other bit of luck happened when I just dropped in at a sale at Sotheby's, Belgravia (now defunct). I sat down literally as a large parian figure of the first man to swim the Channel, Captain Webb, was held up. My instinct was to buy it but I refrained (I should not have). However, when the next parian figure, raised aloft by the porter, was seen to be holding a tennis racket and reminded me very much of an early photograph of Willie Renshaw, I bid for and got it. It proved to be dated 1884, the year that Renshaw won the title for the fourth time in his record six successive wins.

I felt that there was only one place for these two objects, and was very glad to present them to the museum. The water colour is still the earliest known painting of a lawn tennis subject and the parian figure probably also the earliest dated piece of its kind. I am always glad to see them whenever I visit the museum, but still disappointed that I have been unable to trace either Strafford Lodge or, with any certainty, the artist. The house was probably, I feel, in the Lake District and the artist could possibly have been Edith Rawnsley, wife of Canon Rawnsley, the first director of the National Trust. Like so many Victorian ladies, she was an accomplished amateur painter but, according to an aged niece of her's whom I tracked down, she very rarely painted a portrait. On 25 April 1877 she and her husband-to-be were either just engaged or about to become so. This would make it a self-portrait (possibly the pair to the one that her niece said she had painted of her husband) and the title 'Match-ball' just right for the challenging look in the girl's eye as she was about to serve. The scent of this picture's provenance may have gone cold but it is a trail I intend to pursue.

However, all that is looking ahead a little. When I found that my broadcasting commitments were becoming fewer and fewer, for a while I flirted with the idea of dealing in Chinese porcelain myself. Eventually I decided to have a go and to see only selected clients at my home. I also decided that I would only deal in good things – pieces that were so desirable that buyers would seek me out, rather than the other way round. I reckoned I had enough capital to buy forty such pieces and, for a start, that seemed just enough.

But another twist of fate played havoc with my rather airy-fairy – even self-satisfied – ideas. By the time I had sorted out my financial affairs the market for Chinese porcelain had risen dramatically and seemed to be zooming higher with every sale. Instead of forty I was able to buy only half a dozen good and perfect pieces. The rest of my stock perforce was good but damaged, or perfect and second-rate, or too common to be really desirable.

Moreover, I soon found that far from seeking me out,

prospective buyers had to be lured and I could not afford to be choosy as to who came to the house. For a while (I suppose while I was a 'fresh' prospect) I did manage to sell a few pieces, but in the process I discovered things about myself. I was not a dealer but at heart always a collector for, if I bought a nice piece for stock, I invariably wanted to keep it. Nor was I a business man. I found it difficult to be hard enough, and poker-faced enough, not to be driven down and down by a tough dealer, who could divine that I desperately wanted a sale. As to 'commission', I found this side of things very difficult. I resented the attitude of some 'professionals', who seemed to think that an introduction merited a commission – not just once but also for any future transactions.

I had made my purchases at what proved to be the very top of the market. In the summer of 1974 two things happened simultaneously that resulted in a dramatic fall in the prices of Chinese porcelain. The first was the bankruptcy of a young dealer, who had made a big splash on the rising market and had interested young turks in the City in Chinese porcelain as an investment portfolio. The second was the Portugese Revolution, which occurred at the precise moment that a well-known dealer had bought a very rare piece at Sotheby's for the then gargantuan record price of £420,000, on behalf of a collector, a Portugese banker, who would only buy at auction and through the dealer concerned. The collector perforce reneged on the deal. How the matter was settled between Sotheby's and the wretched dealer I know not, but the two unhappy coincidental events precipitated a collapse in the market, from which it has never fully recovered.

Whereas in the great boom of 1972/73 damaged and second-rate pieces were commanding good prices on the coat-tails of the good and perfect ones, now nobody wanted them. The market for the best and perfect things eventually recovered, but anything else always seems to meet with uncertainty and hesitancy – and only edges up in price very slowly. It was in this climate that I made my inadequate and amateurish sortie into the hard world of dealing, and it was not long before I had to call it a day. The antique sands had buried me without trace. I only surfaced again as a collector in response to the lure of the Hatcher seventeen century junk salvage.

While all this was going on another very significant event had occurred in our lives. The Womble phenomenon. It all happened like this. From the start of our marriage Liza had been writing – mainly children's books but also short stories, romantic novels, articles and so on. She had as well done a lot of freelance broadcasting. She is a prolific writer and many of her children's books had made their mark, particularly a series of magic books (all had 'Magic' in their title), which many critics ranked with E. Nesbit's. But *The Wombles*, published in 1969, broke all bounds.

They came to life as the germ of an idea in the autumn of 1968, when John Denton, the managing editor at Ernest Benn's, for whom Liza had already written, rang her up and said, 'Liza, I want you to find the answer to Paddington Bear. Think about it.' 'Oh, I will,' she said. Popping the request into her mental computer, she promptly let it sink to the bottom under the pressure of immediate demands on her busy life. Just before Christmas the phone went and John's voice asked, 'Well, Liza?' 'Well, what?' replied Liza defensively. 'The answer to Paddington Bear, of course.' 'Oh that!' said Liza desperately. 'It's coming.'

On Boxing Day, which was fine and crisp, Liza took Kate and Marcus, then thirteen and eight, up to Wimbledon Common to escape from the bosom of the family, which had included my parents and two elderly cousins for Christmas lunch. 'Go on, run around and make as much noise as you like,' she said, letting them off the leash. Meanwhile, hands in pockets, she was pacing up and down, struggling with the birthpangs of an idea. Suddenly Kate, with glowing cheeks and frosted breath, ran up to her, crying out, 'Oh, Mummy, isn't it wonderful here on Wombledon Common?' 'That's it!' exclaimed Liza, seizing on inspiration and soon the whole idea had crystallised in a two-page breakdown of *The Wombles*, their characteristics and their home in the Wimbledon Burrow.

The two children were at school in Broadstairs but their Easter half terms were a week apart. I had to come back for work, leaving Liza in our hotel room with her 'triper' (as she always called her typewriter), a pile of paper, her Womble synopsis and a bottle of whisky. When I returned next weekend, the book and the bottle were nearing their ends. A quick read through and I immediately had that feeling of recognition that any good work of art engenders. I knew without doubt that here was a classic in the line of AA Milne and Kenneth Grahame.

The rest is Womble history. The TV films and the music of Mike Batt, combined with Liza's brilliant and very endearing character-isation, ensured what was then a record runaway success. Liza had indeed found the answer to Paddington Bear, though he and other characters have since benefited tremendously from the exploits of the Womble pioneers.

Everyone thought that *The Wombles* had made Liza a very rich woman. They did not realise how many other interested parties were involved – some of them with very sticky fingers. That said, there was quite a nice income from the merchandising for a few years while, in the words of a colleague full of barrow-boy optimism, *The Wombles* were 'a licence to print money'. This was offsetting my failure to generate income, either from antique dealing or from broadcasting. It also enabled us to keep up our home in Spencer Park (that unique nineteenth century development, by the Lord Spencer of the day, on Wandsworth Common) in the manner to which it had been accustomed.

Even so, the bulk off this welcome income was going down the fiscal drain, and with even better times in sight, our accountant and I were both trying to convince Liza that a chance like this would never come again and that it was foolish not to move to a less tax-hungry place. Liza had always hated moves. She had not really wanted to leave our old home of twenty years in Earlsfield Road, for Spencer Park. Once established there, she utterly loved it and was adamantly against moving. At last, but as it turned out too late, she was persuaded. However, she refused to go anywhere except to her beloved Alderney, where she, Kate and Marcus had enjoyed their holiday home for so long. We were first going in 1977 but the alterations necessary to the Alderney house, if we were going to live there, were far from complete, so removal was put off by a year. In the two-year interim between the decision and our going, the Womble boom had climaxed and was fast evaporating. The move to Alderney had become irrevocable but the financial benefit to be derived from it had been almost entirely extinguished.

The move to Alderney proved for me to be a disaster. I had known it for years – ever since Liza had gone there on holiday with the children. At her behest I had paid a lightning visit and, in my first impression, had fallen for the behind-the-times charm of what seemed to be an enchanted island. But I had never spent long there, not being a swimmer, surfer, golfer, bird-watcher, sailor, or interested in any of the other activities the island boasted.

Now I was to discover that Alderney is the sort of place that polarises people and relationships. You are either of it and by, with or from it – or not. You cannot be indifferent to it. Liza is an extrovert who became more so, loving the community life and

152

gelling perfectly with it. The island loved her and she the island. I am introvert by nature, though my BBC work had made me better at meeting people and perhaps appearing superficially extrovert. Now I reverted to type and, with nothing congenial to occupy me, became more and more of a recluse.

In our Alderney eyrie I felt more and more cut off from the antique world and I was getting most depressed. With no work of any significance, I was becoming increasingly frustrated and isolated. There had been strains betwen Liza and me for some time. I knew she would never leave her adored Alderney and for my part I was feeling ever more certain that I must get away. So our parting was agreed, with sadness and regret for so much. Thirty-five years and two children are a great deal to have in common. We are still very good friends and as I'm now not far away, in Guernsey, I'm sure we always will be.

EPILOGUE
THE NANKING CARGO

M Y INTEREST IN CHINESE PORCELAIN HAS PLAYED A SIGNIFICANT PART IN SHAPING MY LIFE, SO PERHAPS IT WAS INEVITABLE THAT at this crucial and difficult moment my spirits should have been revived by an extraordinary man and an extraordinary venture. Just before I left Alderney I received a catalogue from Christie's, Amsterdam, of a sale to be held on St Valentine's Day in 1984. On its front the catalogue had a colour photograph of a remarkable blue and white cat nightlight, with the legend underneath:

FINE AND IMPORTANT

LATE MING

AND TRANSITIONAL PORCELAIN

Recently recovered from an Asian vessel in the South China Sea
The Property of Captain Michael Hatcher

I rang a friend, Colin Sheaf, in the oriental department at Christie's to find out more. He was very enthusiastic, having catalogued it himself. Since it was of the Transitional period between the Ming and Ching dynasties, it was my specialist field of collecting. I decided to go and try my luck in Amsterdam.

The first sight of the row upon row of blue and white vases, jars,

154

boxes and covers, dishes of all sizes, wine cups, rice wine bottles, etc was staggering – and daunting in prospect to view properly. And all this – in the first sale some six and a half thousand pieces – had been salvaged in extraordinary conditions from the seabed. Fortunately, many of the big dealers and collectors did not attend the sale, for nobody felt that pieces, even though perfect otherwise as nearly all of them were, whose glaze had been affected by sea minerals could possibly have any real value. How wrong they proved to be, for the effect on the glaze was to soften it, so that under it the blue, instead of having a brilliant and comparatively glaring lustre, now had a charm of its own like a faded tapestry.

The saleroom went wild. Estimates, which Christie's had wisely kept very modest, were easily exceeded in every case and the bidding was highly competitive. A record in itself was that every lot was sold. Those attending realised that they were in a sense privileged to be seeing so much of this porcelain which, if it had ever reached Amsterdam at its appointed mid-seventeenth century date, would have been auctioned off on the quayside. They realised, too, that there was a quite extraordinary romantic provenance to this collection, which totalled 23,000 pieces, with two more sales yet to come.

In all, there were more than a thousand different shapes and designs, made literally on the 1644 borderline of Ming and Ching. There were two box-covers dated 1643 and many of the larger jars and covers and vases were so typical of known dated pieces of about 1640, that the consensus of expert opinion became certain that the Chinese junk, from which they had been salvaged must have sunk in about 1645. The variety, and the fact that many types were either unknown or the earliest example of their kind, made this haul of fascinating interest to scholars and collectors of the period.

Although prices were extraordinarily high, they would un-doubtedly have been far higher if this treasure of Chinese porcelain had received the same worldwide publicity that the second Hatcher salvage 'The Nanking Cargo' attained. True, the blue and white porcelain in 'The Nanking Cargo' had on the whole been almost pristinely preserved by the ship's main cargo of tea, a much more valuable commodity in those days. But the wares consisted almost entirely of dinner and tea services of well-known type and pattern. The cargo of the mid-seventeenth century Chinese junk was far more intrinsically interesting and of greater value to collectors.

I was lucky to be in at the beginning and managed to come away with quite a few treasures. The prize that I am proudest of was a unique group of little vases that were sold together in one lot. They are beautifully painted, clearly by the same hand, and of the highest quality. Two big dealers fought it out. They had gone well beyond the estimate. I coveted those vases but I had no intention of competing. To my astonishment, as the bidding stoped and the auctioneer, well satisfied already, was giving a cursory last look round, I felt my arm – as if on a puppet string – being impelled upwards. Looking at me incredulously, the auctioneer uttered the price. In the silence that followed I could feel my heart thumping. Neither of the two dealers said a word and he brought the hammer down. I was horrified at what I had done, quite unable to understand what had caused the madness. It wasn't long before I was very glad, for I realised that I had come away with one of the best lots in the sale.

That sale having gone so well, Christie's decided to put the remainder, some 16,000 pieces, up the following June in time to catch the big London antique fairs. Dealers had sold off their purchases of the first sale so fast that the second went even better, again every lot being sold. I only managed to get one or two that time. The final sale was in February 1985 when, as a result of his home in Singapore having been burgled, Mike Hatcher decided to sell his own collection from the salvage. There were only 400 pieces this time and everybody scrambled for them.

After the first day of the sale I did an enthusiastic piece first on *Today*. Hearing this, a television producer on the now defunct *Sixty Minutes* evening programme, interviewed Mike and showed some of his pieces. This was the first publicity he had had and, taken with the success of the sales, it ensured that when the sale of 'The Nanking Cargo' was announced Christie's were in a position to beat the drum and the world's media responded. I was able to do a half-hour radio News 'special' programme on his story and the difficulty of locating the wreck. His was a fascinating tale which, since I knew him fairly well by now, I was able to extract.

He was born in York and at an early age was put in the care of Dr Barnardo's Orphanage in Sussex. When he was thirteen they sent him out to Australia to their home and farm in New South Wales. He grew up learning fast in a very hard school. 'I never lost a fight,' he told me, not so much with pride as matter-of-factly. It wasn't long before this tough little Pommy (and there were many adjectives added) was looked upon with considerable respect – a good friend but a bad enemy.

He had tremendous experience as a young man, anything and everything from breaking in brumbies (the Australian wild horses) in the outback, to heavy construction work of all kinds and even the girls' pin-up as a Bondi beach-guard. Deciding to sail singlehanded round the world, he was diverted near New Guinea by coming across a group of salvage men working on a World War II Japanese destroyer. He joined them for a while, learned the rudiments and went on to Singapore. Having persuaded the construction company he was working for to start sea salvage, he soon had the experience to form his own company and dived for anything from gold to whisky.

His first find of Chinese porcelain grossed £2 million and gave him the wherewithal to go on prospecting. 'The Nanking Cargo' was the result. That grossed £10 million. 'I want to be the Cousteau of salvage', he declares. And I'm sure he will be. Museums and collectors of Chinese porcelain round the world await his next find. He has started a new chain of collectors, who love the romance and are glad to be sure of the provenance. Personally, I am convinced that there is much more to be heard of Hatcher and much more lost treasure that he will reveal to the world. I certainly will follow his progress eagerly, for I believe that in his own way this extra-ordinary man will continue to astonish with the treasures he brings up from the deep. What will he surface with next?

Hatcher gives me antique hope for the future and so does Channel Television. Bob Evans is the go-ahead producer I work with there, in charge now of their new department making programmes and videos for sale to other companies. The beauty of working with Channel TV is that they are a skilful, compact band of brothers (and sisters), each of whom knows he is an integral part of a small but great team. And the programme is all that matters. We've just finished a mini series of quarter-hour programmes for Channel Four, each with a Sotheby expert on his own specialist subject. The enthusiasm and approach has been like the old days and it has been a joy to work with them.

Perhaps, to end, I should try a little reflection. When I went out to Papua as a young man it was because I wanted to gain experience. Looking back now I believe that I haven't used experience properly – reading, marking, learning and profiting by it. Too often I've repeated a mistake. I have failed conspicuously in two marriages and the fatherhoods that followed; in trying to get my 'wings', and to capitalise on so many 'if only' chances that have come my way.

But I have learnt a couple of things that I believe in firmly – tips that I gladly pass on to you, the reader. The first is: don't be in a hurry to grow up. I certainly haven't yet and probably never will. For me life began again at seventy and the fires are burning as brightly as ever. The second is: life's much more interesting if it's unpredictable. Sufficient unto the morrow. It's rather like opening the door of an antique shop, for you never know what may turn up.

INDEX

Abdessalam, Robert 13
Ablack, Ken 51
Abrahams, Harold, Sybil 68
Adam, Kenneth 135
Adams, Dawn 113
Adams, Godfrey 84, 88
Adelston, Mick 81
Alston, Rex 1, 8, 9, 10, 66, 68
Altweg, Jeanette 96
Andrews, Eamonn 76
Anger, Matt 17
Anne, Princess 118
Antiques Roadshow 147
Arlott, John 83, 145
Arnell, 'Skipper' 50, 71
Ashe, Arthur 5
Asher, Jane 145
Attenborough, David 109, 131
Austin, Mrs Ada 104

Bagnall, Frank 129
Bailey, Kenneth 103
Baird, Colonel 22, 25
Bannister, Roger 84, 116
Barclay, Edmund 32
Barker, Colin 65, 66
Barnett, Isobel 145

Barsley, Michael 107, 108
Batt, Mike 151
Baverstock, Donald 108
Baxter, Raymond 76, 80
Beamish, Tony 40
Becker, Boris, 7, 16–19
Belfer, Maurice 72
Bennett, Leo 65, 66
Bentine, Michael 145
Beresford, Elizabeth (Liza) 56, 78,
    79, 98–100, 118–120, 129, 130,
    133, 134, 147, 150–153
Betz, Pauline 5
Bevin, Ernest 87
Blankers-Koen, Fanny 69
Boddey, Martin 89
Booker, Michael 126
Borg, Bjorn 5
Borotra, Jean 10
Brabazon, Lord 59
Brake, Brian 120, 121
Brasher, Chris 84, 119
Brooks, Roy 109
Bromwich, John 32, 67, 68
Brooke-Taylor, Tim 145
Brown, Carole 139
Bruton, Knowles 137

159

Buckmaster, Maurice 44
Bueno, Maria 6
Burgoyne, Eric 22, 24
Burnham, Forbes 133
Burrows, Bob 14–16
Burt, Jim 22, 24
Bush House ('Bush') 48
Butler, Evelyn 100
Button, Dick 58

Calvert, Phyllis 145
Camacho, George 73
Cameron, James 20
Casson, Hugh 71
Cazalet, Victor 42, 43, 46
Chamberlain, Nevill 41
Charles, Prince 118
Charlie, Bonny Prince 20
Chataway, Chris 84, 116
Chave, Alf 10–12
Chesnut, Ches 89
Churchill, Sir Winston 55, 94, 95
Clarke, Bertie 51, 66
Coats, Col. Jimmie 59
Coleman, David 121-3
Collings, Gp. Capt 62
Come to the Caribbean 134
Connolly, Maureen (Little Mo) 6,
    17, 106
Connors, Jimmie 5
Constantine, Leary 51, 52
Cooper, Duff 43
Cornes, Jack 58, 124
Court, Margaret 6
Cowgill, Brian 124
Cozens, Bert 72
Crawford, Jack 32
Craxton, Anthony 65, 80, 82, 93
Craxton, Anne 66
Cresta, The 59
Crowther, Leslie 144
Curteis, Capt. Gerald 93, 94
Cushing, Peter 144
Cyclops 4

Dalby, Barrington 75, 76
de Coubertìn, Baron Pierre 126
Delaney 116
Denis, Armand & Michele 131
Denmark, King and Queen of 86
Denton, John 151
Dexter, Ted 145
de Lotbiniere, Anthony 112
de Lotbiniere, Seymour (Lobby)
    45–48, 57, 73, 75, 76, 80, 93,
    112, 137
Dimbleby, Richard 75, 83, 92, 94,
    106, 113
Dimmock, Peter 92, 96, 116–119
Disney, Walt 73, 74
Dixon, Robin 126
Dod, Lottie 14
Dog on the Tucker Box 130
Dougall, Robert 40
Drobny, Jaroslav 5, 8
du Boulay, Anthony 143
Duchess, The destroyer 95
du Pont, Margaret (see Osborne)
Dyall, Valentine 145

Edinburgh, The Duke of 88–90
Edelston, Maurice 15
Edwards, Margaret 120
Effie, 112, 113
Elizabeth, Princess 88–91
Elizabeth, Queen 88–91
Elliott, Herb 123
Emerson, Roy 5
Emett, Roland 112, 113
Evans, Bob 157
Evans, Richard 15
Evert-Lloyd, Chris 6
Ewart, George 47

Falkenburg, Bob 67, 68
Falkenburg, Jinx 67
Fidlin 22, 24–26
Fielding, Fenella 145
Finlay, Huck 36, 38, 119

Follit, Renée 20
Fleming, Peter 9
Flynn, Errol 61
Fox, Paul 84, 114, 115, 119–122, 135
Fraser, Neale 5
Fraser, Lady Antonia 145
Furness, John 107

Gardner, James 72
George V King 42
George VI, King 88, 90, 91
Gibson, Althea 6
Gilbert, Joan 79
Glendenning, Raymond 9, 10, 76
Gloucester, The Duke of 93, 95
Godfree, Biddy 148
Going for a Song, 136–45
Gonzales, Pancho 5, 106
Graham, Billy 104
Grahame, Kenneth 151
Grinham, Judy 120
Grinnell-Milne, Duncan 41
Grisewood, Freddie 9, 10, 45
Grisewood, Harmon 39
Gullikson, Tom 15
Gullikson Twins, The 9

Handley, Tommy 44
Hanrott 22, 24
Harper, Jack 13
Hart, Doris 5, 115
Hartwig, Rex 7
Hastie, Rob 16
Hatcher, Capt. Mike 150, 154–7
Hawes, Curtis 105
Hawes, Stanley 129
Hewitt, Bob 16
Hibberd, Stewart 41, 42
Hides, Viv 23
Hill, Graham 145
Hitler, Adolf 41, 43, 47
Hoad, Lew 5, 7, 105
Hopman, Harry 5

Hutchens, Minnie 32

Ingrid, Queen (see Denmark)
Irving, John 136, 137, 141
I.T.M.A. 43, 44

Jackson, Graham 22
Jackson, J. Hampden 52, 53
Janes, Christine, see Truman
Jazy, Michel 123
Jedrezejowska, Jadwiga (Jed) 46
Johnston, Brian 48
Jones, Andrew Miller 102, 107
Jones, Ann 6
Jones, Peter 15

Kent, Princess Marina, Duchess of 8
Kent, The Duchess of 16
Kent, The Duke of 16
Key Flats 109
Killy, Jean-Claude 125
King, Bill 99, 100
King, Billie-Jean 6
King, John 137, 141
Kingbull, Cdr E. J. 41
Kramer, Jack 4, 106
Kukukukus 27
Kwakurra 27

Lambert Chambers, Mrs 14
Lambeth Fire Brigade, 97
Lancaster, Osbert 145
Larsen, Ernst 119
Laver, Rod 5
Lawson, Henry 32
Lendl, Ivan 7, 16, 17
Lenglen, Suzanne 14
Lerwill, Sheila 115
Liddell, Alvar 41, 42, 44
Liddell, Eric 68
Lindwall, Ray 11–13
Lister, Moira 145
Lloyd, David 16

Lloyd-James David 41
Lloyd-James, Professor 41
Loren, Sophia 113
Lothian, Lord 43
Lovelock, Jack 58
Lunn, Sir Arnold 57
Lyttelton, Humphrey 145

Macaulay, Duncan 1
MacDonald, Flora 20
MacPherson, Stewart 9, 48, 75, 76
Manning, Jim 52
Mapu 25
Maritime A.A. 47
Maritime R.A. 47
Marson, Lionel 41
Martin, Jonathan 125
Mary, Queen 14, 86
Maskell, Dan 10, 11, 97
Massimo, Prince 113
Mawson, John 22, 24
Max-Muller, Charles 80, 98
Mayhew, Christopher 52
Mayhew, Patrick 52
Mayotte, Tim 17
McEnroe, John 5, 9, 15
McGivern, Cecil 102
McGrath, Vivian 32, 67
McGregor, Bobby 124
McGregor Mr 40
McKay, Angus 54, 55, 81
McKane, Kitty (see Godfree)
McLeod, Joseph 41
McMillan, Frew 16
Menzies, Dame Patti 130
Mercer, David 15
Merinat M. 58, 61–63
Miall, Leonard 108, 110
Mikes, George 72
Mikhelsen, André 49
Miles, Bernard 145
Miller, Keith 12, 13
Mills, Alan 3
Milne, A.A. 151

Milne, Alasdair 109, 110
Mitchel, Leslie 79
Mithras 113
Mo, Little (see Connolly)
Molotov M. 73
Moore, Gladys 29, 30, 37, 40
Morse, Charles 100
Morundah 130, 131
Mottram, Tony 13
Mountbatten, Earl of Burma 2
Muggeridge, Malcolm 103–105
Munoz, Félipé 125
Mussolini, Benito 39, 41

Nash, Tony 126
Navratilova, Martina 6
Negus, Arthur 136–138, 140, 141,
   143, 144
Newcombe, John 5
Newman, Michael 139
Noble, Ronnie 115–117

O'Connor, Terry 123
Orr-Ewing, Ian 58, 59, 69
Osborne, Margaret 5
Owens, Jessie 69

Paddington Bear 151
Pagan, George 136
Page, Cyril 96
Paish, Geoff 13
Panorama 102–13
Parker, Gibson 40, 48
Parker, Lt. Cdr Michael 90
Parsons, Nicholas 145
Pasarell, Charlie 5
Patch, Miss 50
Paterson, 'Banjo' 130
Paterson, Floyd 118
Patricia, The Trinity House Vessel
   93, 94
Patty, Budge 5, 8
Peacock, Michael 108
Pelly, Blake 33

Perry, Fred 10, 16
Peters, Jim 115, 116
Petra, Yvon 4
Phillips, Frank 41, 42
Phillips, Len 66
Picture Page 79, 102
Pius XII, Pope 38, 39
Power, Black 126
Pratt, Betty 7
Proops, Marjorie 145
Pryor, Addie 117, 118
Pym, Mr 44

R.A.I. 38
Ramsay, Dr Archbishop of
  Canterbury 20
Rawes, Clive 105
Rawnsley, Canon 149
Rawnsley, Edith 149
Reid, Owen 129, 131, 133
Reiff, Gaston 69
Reith, Sir John 44
Renshaw, Willie 149
Renwick, Guy 126
Ricono, Charles 72
Riefenstahl, Leni 58
Riggs, Bobby 43
Rinkl, Ivo 13
Robertson, Kate 151
Robertson, Marcus 118, 151
Robertson, Marian 20
Roe, Isobel 61
Roetter, Charles 59
Rose, Mervyn 7
Rosewall, Ken 5, 7, 8
Rovers 129
Rozfnoi, Sandor 119
Russell, Audrey 80

Sarney, Harvey 71
Schollander, Don 124
Scott, Barbara Anne 58, 96
Scott, Peter 71
Scriven, Peggy 45

Sedgman, Frank 5
Shaw, Bernard 49, 73
Shead, Ann 13
Sheaf, Colin 154
Simon M. 72
Simpson & Galton 112
Six Days to Sydney 130
Smith, Alan 126
Smith, Berkeley 77, 78
Smith, Stan 5
Snagge, John 42, 45, 84, 88–90
Spencer, Lord 152
Sphairistike 148
Spitz, Mark 125
Staley, Jennifer 105, 106
Standing, Michael 45
Stiegler, Josef 123, 124
Strafford Lodge 148, 149
Stringer, Mrs 105
Suttor, Nancy 27, 30, 33, 36–39,
  48
Syrop, Konrad 58, 73

Talbot, Godfrey 88
Tatura Sheep Station 129, 131
Television Sports Club 114
Television Sports Magazine 114
Thetis, H.M.S. 41
Thomas, Sir Miles 128
Thompson, Corey 88
Thorn, Jim 3
Tinling, Ted 3, 105
Trant, Ion 132, 133
Trevaskis, Jim 129
Troke, Clifford 54
Truman, Christine 7, 9, 16

Unwin, Stanley 71

Van Swol, Hans 13, 79
Van Swol, Valerie 79
Vaughan-Thomas, Wynford 45,
  48, 80, 83, 86, 87, 92, 97, 98
Venables, Peter 39
Vizard, John 'Viz' 71

Von Cramm, Gottfried 43

Wade, Robin 147
Wade, Steve 77, 78, 112
Wade, Virginia 6
Walker, Harry 122, 124
Ward, Edward 41
Wassai 25
Watts, Denis (Watto) 31, 32
Webb, Capt. Matthew 149
Weeks, Alan 127
Wells, Alan 68
Wetherell, Virginia 144
Whitehouse, Mrs Mary 106
Whitefield, Mal 69
Wicks, Jim 54
Widdows, Robin 126

Williams, Gerry 15
Wills, Helen 148
Wilson, Peter 54
Wingfield, Major Walter Clopton
    148
Wint, Arthur 69
Wogai 25
Woodroffe, Tommy 45
Wombles, The 151
Wurmser, Alfred 99, 107
Wyndham-Goldie, Grace 108, 109

York, Duke and Duchess of 90,
    91

Zatopek, Emil 68, 69, 115–117
Zivojinovic, Slobadan 17, 46

Pst —

Arthur Negus went off with my Key! May I leave my things here 'till they find me something Else.